Projects for Microsoft® Windows® 95

Brief Edition

Gary R. Brent
Scottsdale Community College

Paul B. Thurrott

The Benjamin/Cummings Publishing Company, Inc.
Menlo Park, California • Reading, Massachusetts
New York • Don Mills, Ontario • Harlow, U.K. • Amsterdam
Bonn • Paris • Milan • Madrid • Sydney • Singapore • Tokyo
Seoul • Taipei • Mexico City • San Juan, Puerto Rico

ISBN 0-8053-1613-2 bundled version
ISBN 0-0853-1618-3 stand alone version
1 2 3 4 5 6 7 8 9 10—DOW—00 99 98 97 96

Senior Editor: *Maureen A. Allaire*
Project Editor: *Kathy G. Yankton*
Assistant Editor: *Heide Chavez*
Executive Editor: *Michael Payne*
Project Manager: *Adam Ray*
Associate Production Editor: *Jennifer Englander*
Marketing Manager: *Melissa Baumwald*
Custom Publishing Operations Specialist: *Michael Smith*
Senior Manufacturing Coordinator: *Janet Weaver*
Composition and Film Manager: *Lillian Hom*
Composition and Film Buyer: *Vivian McDougal*
Manufacturing Supervisor: *Casi Kostecki*
Copy Editor: *Barbara Conway*
Proofreader: *Holly McLean Aldis*
Indexer: *Mark Kmetzko*
Text-Designer: *Mark Ong*
Cover Design: *Yvo Riezebos*

Ordering from the SELECT System

For more information on ordering and pricing policies for the SELECT System of microcomputer applications texts and their supplements, please contact your Addison-Wesley •Benjamin/Cummings sales representative or call our SELECT Hotline at 800/854-2595.

The Benjamin/Cummings Publishing Company, Inc.
2725 Sand Hill Road
Menlo Park, CA 94025
http://www.aw.com/bc/is
bc.is@aw.com

Getting Started

Welcome to the *SELECT Lab Series*. We invite you to explore how you can take advantage of the newest Windows 95 features of the most popular software applications using this up-to-date learning package.

Greater access to ideas and information is changing the way people work. With Windows 95 applications you have greater integration capabilities and access to Internet resources than ever before. The *SELECT Lab Series* helps you take advantage of these valuable resources with special assignments devoted to the Internet and additional connectivity resources which can be accessed through our web site, **http://www.aw.com/bc/is.**

The key to using software is making the software work for you. The *SELECT Lab Series* will help you learn to use software as a productivity tool by guiding you step-by-step through case-based projects similar to those you will encounter at school, work, or home. When you are finished with this learning package, you will be fully prepared to use the resources this software offers. Your success is our success.

A Guided Tour

To facilitate the learning process, we have developed a consistent organizational structure for each module in the *SELECT Lab Series.*

You begin using the software almost immediately. A brief **Overview** introduces the software package and the basic application functions. **Getting Help** covers the on-line Help feature in each package. **A Note to the Student** explains any special conventions or system configurations observed in a particular module.

Each module contains six to eight **Projects,** an **Operations Reference** of all the operations covered in each module, an extensive **Glossary** of **key terms,** and an **Index.**

The following figures introduce the elements you will encounter as you use each SELECT module.

PROJECT 2: BUILDING A LARGER WORKSHEET

OBJECTIVES

After completing this project, you will be able to:

- Move a cell
- Check the spelling of worksheet data
- Use preselected ranges for data entry
- Copy the contents of a cell
- Use relative cell references in formulas
- Use the @SUM @function and the Sum SmartIcon

Each project begins with **Learning Objectives** that describe the skills and commands you will master.

CASE STUDY: SALES OF AUDIO RECORDINGS

From 1975 to 1990, the popularity of the kinds of media used for recorded music shifted dramatically. These changes are illustrated in Figure 2.1.

	A	B	C	D	E	F	G
1	Shipments of Audio Recordings						
2	(in millions of dollars)						
3		1975	1980	1985	1990		
4	Phonograph Records						
5	LP Albums	1485	2290.3	1280.5	86.5		
6	Singles	211.5	269.3	281	94.4		
7	Total Records	?	?	?	?		
8	Tapes						
9	8-tracks	583	526.4	25.3	0		
10	Cassettes	98.8	776.4	2411.5	3472.4		
11	Total Tapes	?	?	?	?		
12	Compact Discs						
13	Regular CDs	0	0	389.5	3451.6		
14	CD Singles	0	0	0	6		
15	Total CDs	?	?	?	?		
16	Grand Total	?	?	?	?		
17							

Figure 2.1

Projects revolve around **Case Studies**, which provide real-world scenarios so you can learn an application in a broader context.

Designing the Solution

In this project, you will build a 1-2-3 worksheet that will calculate the totals indicated by the question marks in Figure 2.1. You will create formulas to calculate totals for each year in each media category (records, tapes, and CDs) and grand totals (the totals of records, tapes, and CDs combined). You will then format the worksheet so the information is optimally readable.

Each topic begins with a brief explanation of concepts you will learn and the operations you will perform.

Designing the Solution introduces you to important problem-solving techniques. You will see how to analyze the case study and design a solution before you sit down at the computer.

The **computer icon** provides a cue that you should begin working at the computer, and **Numbered steps** guide you step-by-step through each project, providing detailed instructions on how to perform operations.

IN-10
INTRODUCTION TO WINDOWS

USING THE CONTROL MENU

When you select the Control menu box in the upper-left corner of a window, the Control menu drops down. If you are using a keyboard, the ***Control menu*** enables you to control window operations, such as moving, sizing, and closing windows. Mouse users perform these operations by clicking, double-clicking, or dragging windows. You can use the Control menu to close any window, including the Program Manager window. By closing the Program Manager window, you will exit Windows, in addition to closing the Program Manager.

To close the active window:

1 Mouse: Click the Control menu box.
or Keys: Press ALT and then press SPACE

Be sure to click the Control menu box only once. Your screen should look like the one in Figure 9.

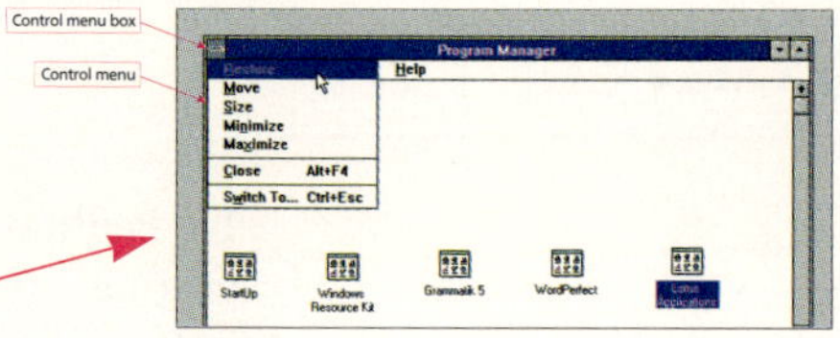

Figure 9

2 Choose Close.

Notice that you get a dialog box to exit Windows.

3 Select Cancel.

Most dialog boxes contain a Cancel button than enables you to cancel a command.

EXIT **If necessary, you can save you file, exit Windows and continue this project later.**

MOVING A WINDOW

Occasionally one window will hide another. A window can be moved by dragging its title bar or by using the Control menu.

Visual cues such as **screen shots** provide examples of what you will see on your own computer screen, reinforce key concepts, and help you check your work.

Exit points identify good places in each project to take a break.

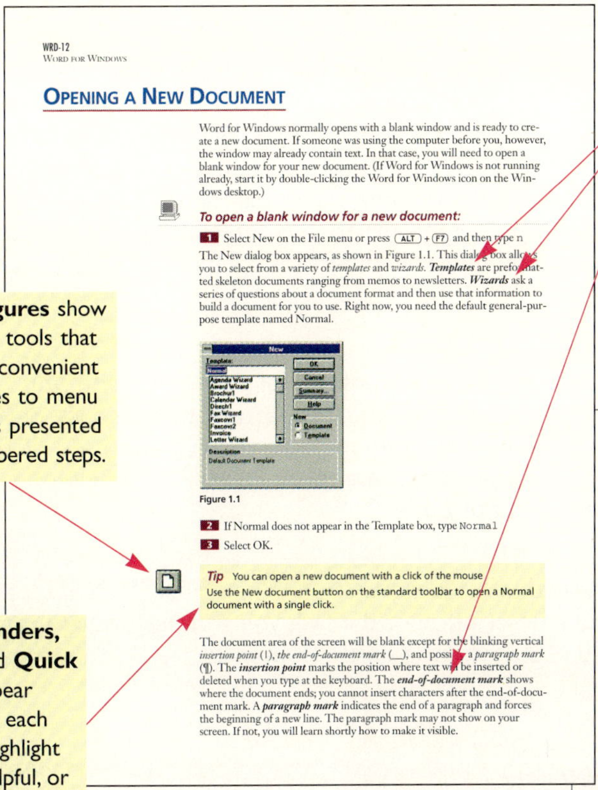

WRD-12
Word for Windows

Opening a New Document

Word for Windows normally opens with a blank window and is ready to create a new document. If someone was using the computer before you, however, the window may already contain text. In that case, you will need to open a blank window for your new document. (If Word for Windows is not running already, start it by double-clicking the Word for Windows icon on the Windows desktop.)

To open a blank window for a new document:

1 Select New on the File menu or press ALT + F7 and then type n

The New dialog box appears, as shown in Figure 1.1. This dialog box allows you to select from a variety of *templates* and *wizards*. ***Templates*** are preformatted skeleton documents ranging from memos to newsletters. ***Wizards*** ask a series of questions about a document format and then use that information to build a document for you to use. Right now, you need the default general-purpose template named Normal.

Figure 1.1

2 If Normal does not appear in the Template box, type `Normal`

3 Select OK.

Tip You can open a new document with a click of the mouse
Use the New document button on the standard toolbar to open a Normal document with a single click.

The document area of the screen will be blank except for the blinking vertical *insertion point* (|), *the end-of-document mark* (_), and possibly a *paragraph mark* (¶). The ***insertion point*** marks the position where text will be inserted or deleted when you type at the keyboard. The ***end-of-document mark*** shows where the document ends; you cannot insert characters after the end-of-document mark. A ***paragraph mark*** indicates the end of a paragraph and forces the beginning of a new line. The paragraph mark may not show on your screen. If not, you will learn shortly how to make it visible.

Key Terms are boldfaced and italicized and appear throughout each project.

Margin figures show on-screen tools that are often convenient alternatives to menu commands presented in the numbered steps.

Tips, Reminders, Cautions, and **Quick Fixes** appear throughout each project to highlight important, helpful, or pertinent information about each application.

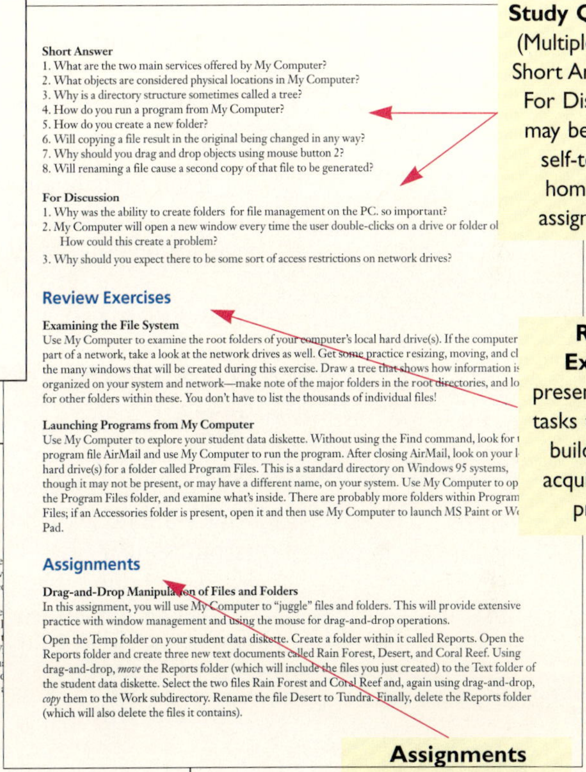

Short Answer

1. What are the two main services offered by My Computer?
2. What objects are considered physical locations in My Computer?
3. Why is a directory structure sometimes called a tree?
4. How do you run a program from My Computer?
5. How do you create a new folder?
6. Will copying a file result in the original being changed in any way?
7. Why should you drag and drop objects using mouse button 2?
8. Will renaming a file cause a second copy of that file to be generated?

For Discussion

1. Why was the ability to create folders for file management on the PC. so important?
2. My Computer will open a new window every time the user double-clicks on a drive or folder ol How could this create a problem?
3. Why should you expect there to be some sort of access restrictions on network drives?

Review Exercises

Examining the File System

Use My Computer to examine the root folders of your computer's local hard drive(s). If the computer part of a network, take a look at the network drives as well. Get some practice resizing, moving, and cl the many windows that will be created during this exercise. Draw a tree that shows how information is organized on your system and network—make note of the major folders in the root directories, and lo for other folders within these. You don't have to list the thousands of individual files!

Launching Programs from My Computer

Use My Computer to explore your student data diskette. Without using the Find command, look for t program file AirMail and use My Computer to run the program. After closing AirMail, look on your l hard drive(s) for a folder called Program Files. This is a standard directory on Windows 95 systems, though it may not be present, or may have a different name, on your system. Use My Computer to op the Program Files folder, and examine what's inside. There are probably more folders within Program Files; if an Accessories folder is present, open it and then use My Computer to launch MS Paint or W Pad.

Assignments

Drag-and-Drop Manipulation of Files and Folders

In this assignment, you will use My Computer to "juggle" files and folders. This will provide extensive practice with window management and using the mouse for drag-and-drop operations.

Open the Temp folder on your student data diskette. Create a folder within it called Reports. Open the Reports folder and create three new text documents called Rain Forest, Desert, and Coral Reef. Using drag-and-drop, *move* the Reports folder (which will include the files you just created) to the Text folder of the student data diskette. Select the two files Rain Forest and Coral Reef and, again using drag-and-drop, *copy* them to the Work subdirectory. Rename the file Desert to Tundra. Finally, delete the Reports folder (which will also delete the files it contains).

Study Questions (Multiple Choice, Short Answer, and For Discussion) may be used as self-tests or homework assignments.

Review Exercises present hands-on tasks to help you build on skills acquired in the projects.

Assignments require critical thinking and encourage synthesis and integration of project skills.

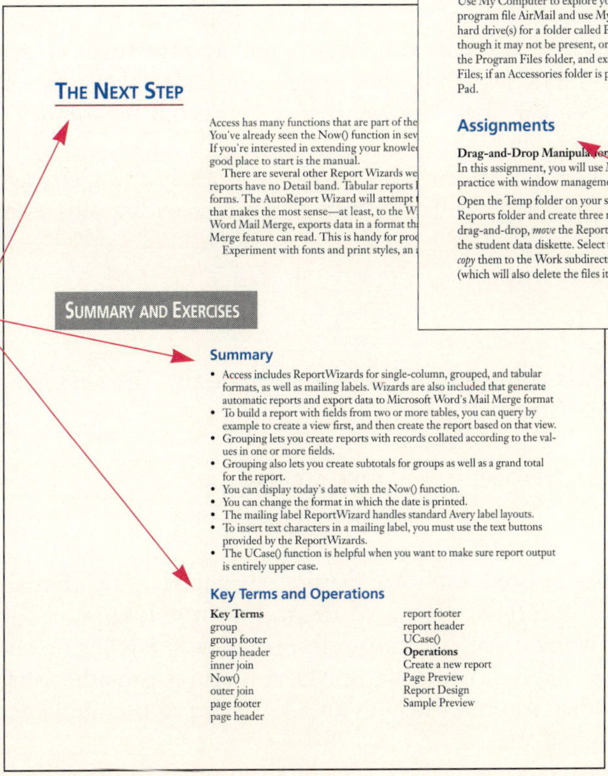

The Next Step

Access has many functions that are part of the
You've already seen the Now() function in sev
If you're interested in extending your knowle
good place to start is the manual.
There are several other Report Wizards we
reports have no Detail band. Tabular reports l
forms. The AutoReport Wizard will attempt t
that makes the most sense—at least, to the W
Word Mail Merge, exports data in a format th
Merge feature can read. This is handy for prod
Experiment with fonts and print styles, an

Summary and Exercises

Summary

- Access includes ReportWizards for single-column, grouped, and tabular formats, as well as mailing labels. Wizards are also included that generate automatic reports and export data to Microsoft Word's Mail Merge format
- To build a report with fields from two or more tables, you can query by example to create a view first, and then create the report based on that view.
- Grouping lets you create reports with records collated according to the values in one or more fields.
- Grouping also lets you create subtotals for groups as well as a grand total for the report.
- You can display today's date with the Now() function.
- You can change the format in which the date is printed.
- The mailing label ReportWizard handles standard Avery label layouts.
- To insert text characters in a mailing label, you must use the text buttons provided by the ReportWizards.
- The UCase() function is helpful when you want to make sure report output is entirely upper case.

Key Terms and Operations

Key Terms
group
group footer
group header
inner join
Now()
outer join
page footer
page header
report footer
report header
UCase()

Operations
Create a new report
Page Preview
Report Design
Sample Preview

Each project ends with **The Next Step** which discusses the concepts from the project and proposes other uses and applications for the skills you have learned, a **Summary,** and a list of **Key Terms and Operations.**

Following the Numbered Steps

To make the application modules easy to use in a lab setting, we have standardized the presentation of hands-on computer instructions as much as possible. The numbered step sections provide detailed, step-by-step instructions to guide you through the practical application of the conceptual material presented. Both keystroke and mouse instructions are used according to which one is more appropriate to complete a task. The instructions in the module assume that you know how to operate the keyboard, monitor, and printer.

Tip When you are using a mouse, unless indicated otherwise, you should assume that you are clicking the left button on the mouse. Several modules provide instructions for both mouse and keyboard users. When separate mouse and keyboard steps are given, be sure to follow one method or the other, but not both.

Each topic begins with a brief explanation of concepts. A computer icon or the ▶ symbol and a description of the task you will perform appear each time you are to begin working on the computer.

For Example:

To enter the address:

1 Type `123 Elm Street` and press ENTER

Notice that the keys you are to press and the text you are to type stand out. The text you will type appears in a special typeface to distinguish it from regular text. The key that you are to press mimics the labels of the keys on your keyboard.

When you are to press two keys or a key and a character simultaneously, the steps show the keys connected either with a plus sign or a bar.

For Example: SHFT + TAB
CTRL + C

When you are to press keys sequentially, the keys are not connected and a space separates them.

For Example: CTRL PGDN
HOME HOME ↑

Be sure to press each key firmly, but quickly, one after the other. Keys begin repeating if you hold them down too long.

In some instances margin figures of single icons or buttons will appear next to the numbered steps. Margin figures provide visual cues to important tools that you can select as an alternative to the menu command in the numbered step.

For typographical conventions and other information unique to the application, please see *A Note to the Student* in the Overview of each module.

The *SELECT* Lab Series—A Connected Learning Resource

The *SELECT Lab Series* is a complete learning resource for success in the Information Age. Our application modules are designed to help you learn fast and effectively. Based around projects that reflect your world, each module helps you master key concepts and problem-solving techniques for using the software application you are learning. Through our web site you can access dynamic and current information resources that will help you get up to speed on the Information Highway and keep up with the ever changing world of technology.

Explore our web site **http://www.aw.com/bc/is** to discover:

- **B/C Link Online:** Our on-line newsletter which features the latest news and information on current computer technology and applications.
- **Student Opportunities and Activities:** Benjamin/Cummings' web site connects you to important job opportunities and internships.
- **What's New:** Access the latest news and information topics.
- **Links:** We provide relevant links to other interesting resources and educational sites.

The TechSuite

This module may be part of our new custom bundled system—the **Benjamin/Cummings TechSuite.** Your instructor can choose any combination of concepts texts, applications modules, and software to meet the exact needs of your course. The TechSuite meets your needs by offering you one convenient package at a discount price.

Supplements

Each module has a corresponding Instructor's Manual with a Test Bank and Transparency Masters. For each project in the student text, the Instructor's Manual includes Expanded Student Objectives, Answers to Study Questions, and Additional Assessment Techniques. The Test Bank contains two separate tests (with answers) consisting of multiple choice, true/false, and fill-in questions that are referenced to pages in the student's text. Transparency Masters illustrate 25 to 30 key concepts and screen captures from the text.

The Instructor's Data Disk contains student data files, answers to selected Review Exercises, answers to selected Assignments, and the test files from the Instructor's Manual in ASCII format.

Acknowledgments

The Benjamin/Cummings Publishing Company would like to thank the following reviewers for their valuable contributions to the *SELECT Lab Series.*

Joseph Aieta
Babson College

Tom Ashby
Oklahoma CC

Bob Barber
Lane CC

Robert Caruso
Santa Rosa Junior College

Robert Chi
California State
Long Beach

Jill Davis
State University of New
York at Stony Brook

Fredia Dillard
Samford University

Peter Drexel
Plymouth State College

Ralph Duffy
North Seattle CC

David Egle
University of Texas,
Pan American

Jonathan Frank
Suffolk University

Patrick Gilbert
University of Hawaii

Maureen Greenbaum
Union County College

Sally Ann Hanson
Mercer County CC

Sunil Hazari
East Carolina University

Bruce Herniter
University of Hartford

Lisa Jackson
Henderson CC

Cynthia Kachik
Santa Fe CC

Bennett Kramer
Massasoit CC

Charles Lake
Faulkner State
Junior College

Ron Leake
Johnson County CC

Randy Marak
Hill College

Charles Mattox, Jr.
St. Mary's University

Jim McCullough
Porter and Chester
Institute

Gail Miles
Lenoir-Rhyne College

Steve Moore
University of
South Florida

Anthony Nowakowski
Buffalo State College

Gloria Oman
Portland State University

John Passafiume
Clemson University

Leonard Presby
William Paterson
College

Louis Pryor
Garland County CC

Michael Reilly
University of Denver

Dick Ricketts
Lane CC

Dennis Santomauro
Kean College of
New Jersey

Pamela Schmidt
Oakton CC

Gary Schubert
Alderson-Broaddus College

T. Michael Smith
Austin CC

Cynthia Thompson
Carl Sandburg College

Marion Tucker
Northern Oklahoma
College

JoAnn Weatherwax
Saddleback College

David Whitney
San Francisco State
University

James Wood
Tri-County
Technical College

Minnie Yen
University of Alaska,
Anchorage

Allen Zilbert
Long Island University

To Alice and Alex—GRB

To my parents, John and Beverly Thurrott—PBT

Contents

OVERVIEW 1

Overview 1
Objectives 1
  A Note to the Student 2
Starting Windows 2
Using the Desktop 3
  Desktop Objects 3
Using the Mouse 5
  Moving the Mouse 5
  Using the Mouse Buttons 5
  Double-Clicking with the Mouse 7
Exiting Windows 8
Using Windows 9
  Windows Components 9
Using Controls 15
Getting Help in Windows 17
  Context-Sensitive Help 17
  The Help Topics Dialog Box 18
The Next Step 20
Summary and Exercises 21
Summary 21
Key Terms and Operations 21
Study Questions 21
  Multiple Choice 21
  Short Answer 22
  For Discussion 22

PROJECT 1: GETTING STARTED WITH WINDOWS 23

Objectives 23
Using the Start Button 23
  Opening the Start Menu 23
  Touring the Start Menu 24
Working with Application Programs 27
  Launching Programs 27
  Using Documents 29
Multitasking with Windows 30
  Using the Taskbar to Switch Between Programs 32
The Next Step 33
Summary and Exercises 34
Summary 34
Key Terms and Operations 34
Study Questions 34
  Multiple Choice 34
  Short Answer 35
  For Discussion 35
Review Exercise 35
  Using the Start Menu 35
Assignment 35
  Multitasking and Window Manipulation 35

PROJECT 2: FILE MANAGEMENT WITH MY COMPUTER AND EXPLORER 36

Objectives 36
Managing Files with My Computer 36
Taking a Closer Look at My Computer 37
  The File System 37
  Files and Folders 38
  Opening Folders 39
Running Programs from My Computer 40
  Navigating through Multiple Windows 40
Manipulating Files and Folders 41
  Creating Files 41
  Creating Folders 43
  Copying FIles and Folders 43
  Moving Files and Folders 45
  Renaming Files and Folders 45
  Deleting Files and Folders 46
  Using Cut, Copy, and Paste with Files 48
Using Windows Explorer 50
  Launching Windows Explorer 50
  Navigating with a Dual-pane Window 51
Changing View Styles for Folder Contents 53
Using the Explorer Toolbar 53
  Toolbar Items 54
The Next Step 55
Summary and Exercises 55
Summary 55
Key Terms and Operations 56
Study Questions 56
  Multiple Choice 56
  Short Answer 57
  For Discussion 57
Review Exercise 57
  Examining the File System 57
Assignments 58
  Dragging and Dropping Files and Folders 58
  Using Cut-and-Paste 58

OPERATIONS REFERENCE 59

GLOSSARY 63

INDEX 65

Overview

Objectives

After completing this Overview, you should be able to:

- Start Windows
- Locate and identify the various components of the Windows desktop
- Manipulate objects with a mouse
- Use windows and controls
- Use Windows Help
- Shut down and log off Windows

The history of computing, though rich in folklore and technical milestones, is still fairly brief. It was not so long ago that interacting with a computer required flipping banks of switches or feeding stacks of punched cards into a hopper to run a program. Today, modern ***operating systems*** provide an interface between the user and the computer that is far more enjoyable and productive.

The primary purpose of an operating system is to shield the user from the complexities of the underlying hardware. It is a testament to the power of software that computers are now far more complicated yet also far easier to use than in the early days of computing. An operating system is itself a program that provides an environment within which other programs, called ***application programs,*** can run. Application programs use a wide variety of features that are built in the operating system to provide a consistent interface to the user. The part of the operating system that you see and interact with, called a ***graphical user interface (GUI),*** is similar on all modern operating systems, allowing the use of a pointing device called a mouse as well as the standard keyboard. GUIs also support the concept of ***windows,*** or overlapping rectangular areas on-screen, each of which can contain its own program, or ***process.*** These programs run independently of each other and allow the user to be more productive.

Windows 95 is the culmination of years of GUI work on the part of Microsoft and features a powerful, advanced user interface, or ***shell.*** The shell allows you to explore the Windows 95 "world" visually in a variety of ways. Windows 95 is highly customizable, meaning that users can configure their systems easily. Windows 95 also runs the most popular software available: software designed for Windows 3.1, the predecessor to Windows 95. In addition to this legacy software, it runs the latest 32-bit software designed specifically for Windows 95. The 32-bit software is faster and more powerful than the 16-bit software required for previous versions of Windows.

Windows 95 is an exciting operating system that bridges the past with today's technical advances. To users of earlier operating systems, Windows 95 is a thrill to work with, full of features that were previously unavailable anywhere.

A Note to the Student

This module assumes that

- Microsoft Windows 95 is installed on the computer you will be using as you work through the projects
- You know your user name and password, if required
- A blank, formatted diskette will be placed in drive A: (your 3½ inch disk drive).

Starting Windows

When you turn on the computer, Windows will be loaded into memory. This is known as booting, or starting, Windows. After some introductory screens, the Windows desktop will appear.

To start Windows:

1 Turn on the computer system.
The message *Starting Windows 95* appears. Then the Windows "splash" screen will appear.

2 If a window appears asking you to type a user name and password, you should do so now.

Using the Desktop

The Windows desktop provides the backdrop for each session you spend with Windows. Microsoft designed the Windows desktop to be a friendly place but it may not seem so at first glance. Don't despair; there is plenty to do and see on the desktop, and soon you will be launching and using application programs. Figure 0.1 shows a typical view of the Windows desktop at startup.

Figure 0.1

> ***Caution*** The Windows desktop on your screen may be different in some ways from the figures in this module. Because Windows is highly customizable, different sites may have changed the system colors, icons, font styles, and other attributes. This module uses the standard setup for all of its figures.

Desktop Objects

All the parts of the desktop you see are called ***objects.*** This generic term refers to any of the "things" that are on the desktop. Windows uses what is called a noun-verb paradigm, where each object is a noun, and any action you can do with an object is a verb. The Windows desktop will include several objects called *icons,* which usually consist of My Computer, Network Neighborhood, Inbox, and Recycle Bin. An ***icon*** is a graphical representation of an object, and as with any object, you can perform unique actions with it.

While you will be learning more about each of these objects in upcoming projects, a quick look at the items that make up the Windows desktop will provide a brief overview.

My Computer

The My Computer icon is like a doorway into the file system of the computer. My Computer offers the user a straightforward way to browse, or maneuver, through the computer's resources. These resources can include floppy, hard, and CD-ROM drives, and system configuration options.

Network Neighborhood

Network Neighborhood is similar to My Computer, allowing you to browse through network resources such as computers and shared printers. Systems that are not connected to a network may not have this icon.

Inbox

Inbox is the icon for Microsoft's powerful Exchange program and may not appear on your desktop. Exchange is used to send and receive electronic mail (e-mail) and faxes. Sites that have installed Microsoft Plus! for Windows 95 will have additional features built into Exchange.

> ***Tip*** A figure next to text or a numbered step, shown above, represents the button or icon you will use. This type of margin figure appears frequently throughout the module.

Recycle Bin

People familiar with the Macintosh computer will immediately recognize that the Windows Recycle Bin is very similar to the Macintosh Trashcan. It provides a place to store deleted files that can later be permanently removed or recovered.

Taskbar

The Taskbar, shown in Figure 0.2, is the gray area that runs along the bottom of the Windows desktop. By default, the Taskbar always remains visible, and it gives the user an easy way to switch between running programs. The Taskbar has a section at the far right called the status area, or the tray notification area, which displays a clock and, depending on how Windows is configured, miniature icons representing utility programs that are always in memory. In Figure 0.2 the status area has two small utilities installed: a volume control for the sound card, and an audio CD player utility program.

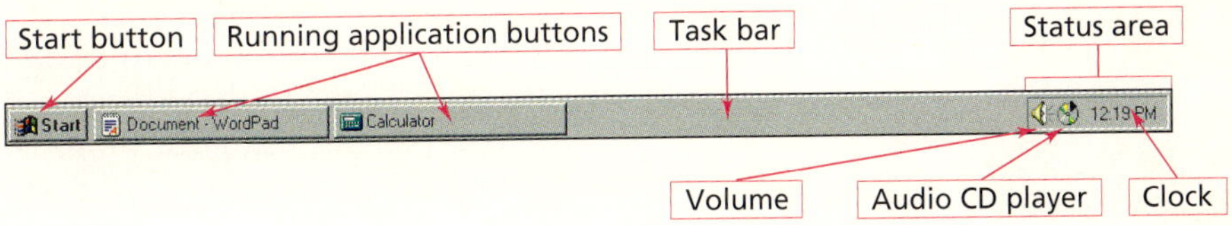

Figure 0.2

The Taskbar also contains the Start button.

Start Button

Located at the far left end of the Taskbar, the Start button provides one-click access to a cascading menu of programs, documents, settings, and other objects. The Start button is designed to provide a direct way for the user to access application programs.

USING THE MOUSE

While it is possible to use Windows without a mouse, doing so is painful at best. A mouse, popularized by the Macintosh computer in the mid-1980s, has become standard equipment on all personal computers and is required to navigate Windows effectively. If you have not had any experience with a mouse, you may find it awkward at first, but using it will soon become second nature.

Moving the Mouse

A mouse is used to move around a small pointer, usually shaped like an arrow, on the screen. The mouse rolls along on a flat surface on a small rubber ball located on its underside. Rolling the ball along the table will cause the pointer on-screen to move—this is how you control the mouse. You should practice moving the mouse now if you are unfamiliar with it.

To move the mouse:

1 Grasp the mouse in your hand.
Your index finger should rest lightly on the leftmost button, and your middle finger should rest on the right button.

2 Move the mouse in a circular motion.
Observe the pointer on-screen as you move the mouse. Try to keep the mouse moving in small, tight circles.

Using the Mouse Buttons

Most PC-compatible mice have two buttons, located at the top of the mouse, that are used to select, or ***click,*** objects. To click an object, you position the pointer over the object and then press and immediately release the mouse button. The ***left mouse button*** is the primary button. Unless a right click is specified, always click with the left button. Clicking an object with the left mouse button selects that object. In Windows, when you click an object with the ***right mouse button*** (right click) you will see on-screen a ***pop-up menu,*** a small free-floating window containing properties and options that are related to that object.

It is time to practice using the mouse buttons. First you will try the left mouse button, which is used to select objects.

To click with the left mouse button:

1 Move the mouse pointer to the icon for My Computer, as shown in Figure 0.3.

Figure 0.3

2 Press and immediately release the left mouse button with your index finger to click the My Computer icon.
The My Computer icon is selected. You can tell that it is selected because its color will change to a blue hue, as shown in Figure 0.4.

Figure 0.4

> ***Tip*** To deselect an object, just click anywhere else on the screen. You will normally want to click somewhere in a blank area of the desktop. If the My Computer icon is selected and you click the Network Neighborhood icon, then the Network Neighborhood icon becomes selected and the My Computer icon is deselected.

3 Practice clicking other icons on the Windows desktop, getting a feel for moving the pointer and for selecting objects with the mouse. When you are done, click the left mouse button anywhere over a blank spot on the desktop to deselect any objects.

Typically, you use the right mouse button to view a pop-up menu for the currently selected object. This menu, sometimes called a context menu, is a small window that lists the various options available for that object. The menu that appears will be slightly different for each object, because each object will have different commands, attributes, and possible actions. The pop-up menu appears next to the current pointer location. A disk drive object, for example, would have options for formatting, disk copying, and other disk-related functions. Almost every object in Windows responds like this to a right-click, including the desktop.

To click with the right mouse button:

1 If My Computer is still selected, click anywhere over a blank spot on the desktop with the left mouse button to deselect My Computer.

2 Click the desktop with the right mouse button.
A pop-up menu appears.

3 Click the My Computer icon with the right mouse button.
The pop-up menu that appears is slightly different than the one that appears when the desktop is clicked with the right mouse button.

Double-Clicking with the Mouse

Although single-clicking the mouse buttons is fairly common, the most common mouse action is ***double-clicking,*** pressing the mouse button twice quickly and then releasing it. Double-clicking is done only with the left mouse button, and it is usually done to open an object. Opening can be different things to different objects. For an application program, opening means launching, or starting, that program. Opening a drive object will actually open a window displaying the contents of the drive.

To double-click:

1 Position the mouse over a blank area of the desktop.

2 Quickly press the mouse button twice in succession to double-click the desktop.
Nothing will actually happen. The desktop is an object that cannot be opened by double-clicking. Most of the time, you will double-click icons.

3 Position the mouse pointer over the My Computer icon and double-click.
Your screen should resemble Figure 0.5.

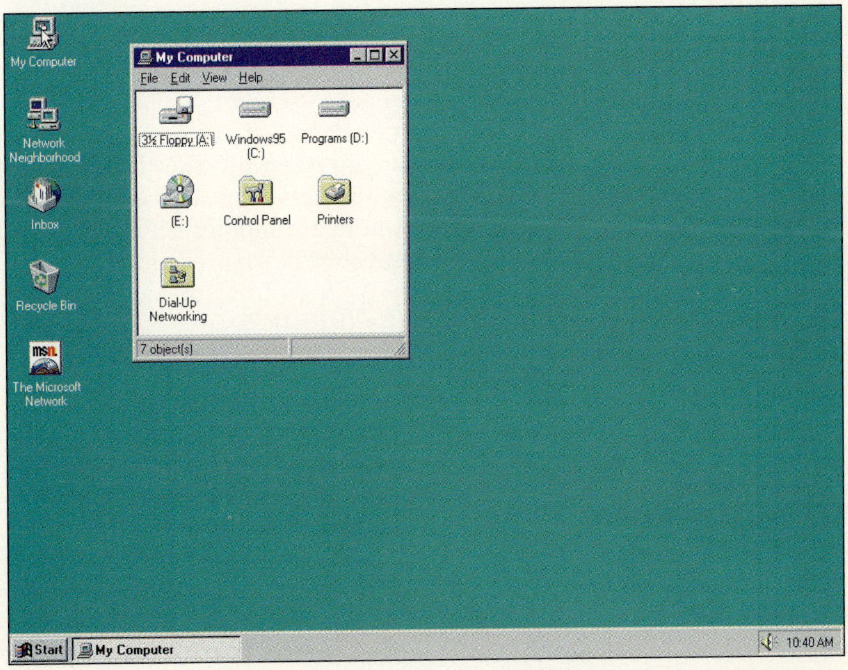

Figure 0.5

Caution Because of the customization options available in Windows, it is possible that your screen does not resemble Figure 0.5. To make your screen more closely follow the standard appearance used in the figures in this module, right-click a blank area in the My Computer window, choose View, and then Large Icons. Also, your My Computer window may show a toolbar of icons under the menu bar that is not seen in the figures. If you would like to turn this off, choose Toolbar from the View menu.

Reminder The distinction between the different mouse clicks is important. A single-click with the left mouse button will *select* an object, a single-click with the right mouse button will *display* a pop-up menu, and a double-click (which is always done with the left mouse button) will *open* an object.

Exiting Windows

Windows requires that you properly shut down the system when you are done using it for the day. Do not turn the PC's power off while Windows is running! This could damage Windows, cause a loss of data, or at the very least leave seemingly random temporary files on the computer's hard drive. Windows is a fairly complex system and needs to do some house-cleaning before it shuts down.

Caution Do not turn off the computer while Windows is running!

Shutting down, or exiting Windows, is straightforward and requires only that you select the Shut Down option from the Start menu. Please note that the following steps will ultimately result in the machine being turned off. In a computer lab environment, it may be preferable to perform a different shut-down procedure.

To exit Windows:

1 Click the Start button on the Taskbar.
The Start menu appears.

2 Select the option titled Shut Down by clicking it with the left mouse button.
The Shut Down Windows dialog box appears, offering you several options.

3 Select *Shut down the computer?,* and then click the Yes button.
Windows is performing its shut-down tasks.

4 Windows will inform you when it is safe to turn off the computer.

Using Windows

One of the major advantages of a graphical user interface is the use of overlapping windows. A window is just a rectangular area of the screen, like a box, that contains a running program or other information.

Window Components

Most windows consist of the same primary components. A component is nothing more than a piece or element of an object. The initial My Computer window, shown in Figure 0.6, contains many common window components (remember that the contents of the window may be slightly different on your computer).

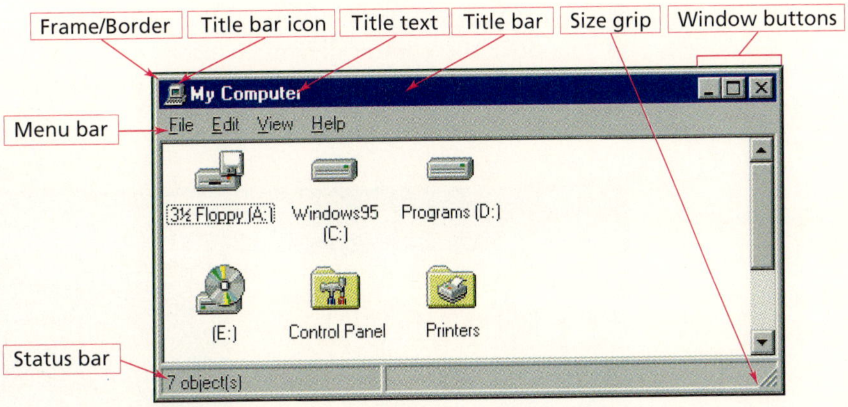

Figure 0.6

Window Frame

Each window has a ***frame,*** or border, that defines the outer edges of that window, as shown in Figure 0.6. In the My Computer window, for example, the window is sizable, meaning that users can resize the window as they see fit. One visual clue that the window is sizable is that it contains a ***size grip*** in the lower-right corner. The size grip is a special handle designed to make resizing (by *dragging*) more obvious to the user.

The action of holding down a mouse button while an object is selected is called ***dragging.*** Like most of the concepts in this Overview, dragging objects with the mouse is a basic Windows skill.

To resize a window:

1 Make sure Windows is running, then open a My Computer window by double clicking the My Computer icon.

2 Position the pointer over the My Computer size grip, as shown in Figure 0.7.
The pointer changes to a diagonal double arrow, indicating that the window can now be resized.

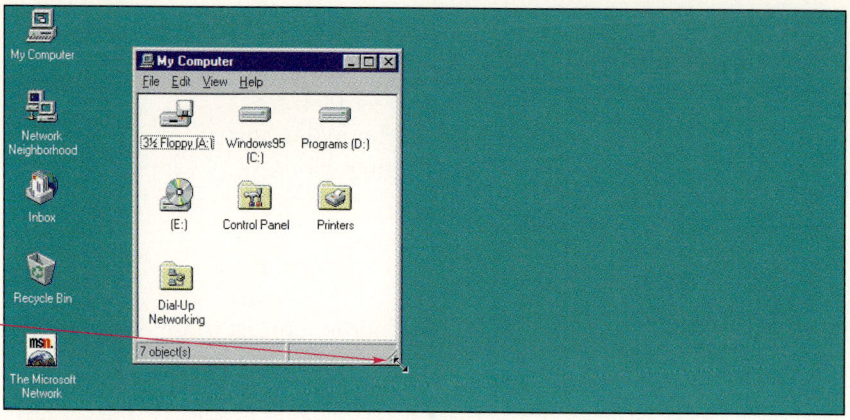

Figure 0.7

3 Drag the size grip by pressing the mouse button and holding it down as you move the pointer diagonally back and forth. A shadow outline of the My Computer window moves with the pointer, as shown in Figure 0.8.

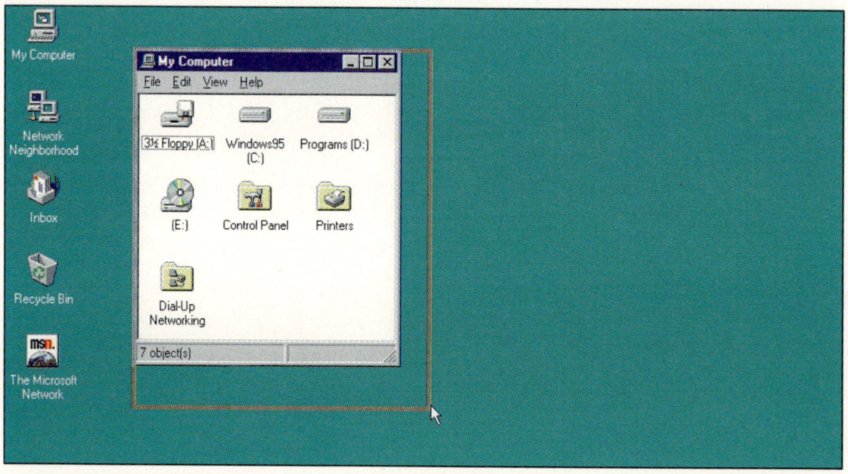

Figure 0.8

The outline shows where the window borders will be when you release the mouse button.

4 Release the mouse button.
The My Computer window is resized.

You may want to experiment with the size grip, sizing the window differently each time and seeing the effect it has.

Title Bar

The title bar is the colored bar along the top edge of a window. It contains a caption, called the ***title text,*** that identifies the window. The title text will duplicate the name of the icon you clicked to open the window. The title bar houses the title bar icons and serves as the primary place for grabbing the window so that it can be dragged (moved) to a new location.

You drag the window by positioning the mouse pointer on the title bar, holding down the left mouse button, and moving the mouse. This dragging action is similar to what you did to resize a window, except that in this case you are dragging the title bar instead of the size grip. You should become comfortable moving windows around with the mouse.

To drag a window with the title bar:

1 Position the mouse pointer over the title bar of the My Computer window, as shown in Figure 0.9.

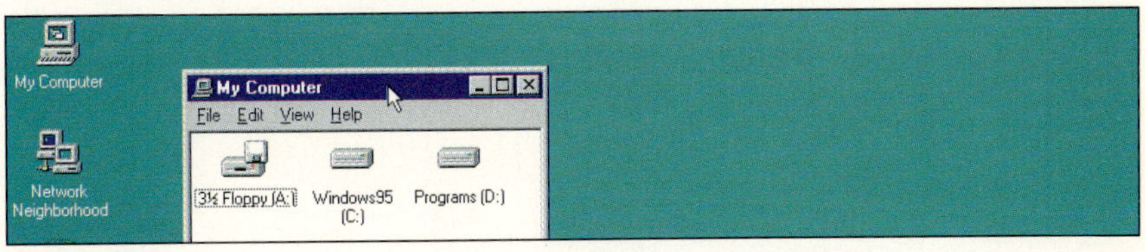

Figure 0.9

2 Drag the My Computer window by pressing and holding down the left mouse button and then moving the mouse in a circular pattern. Again, a shadow outline of the window moves with the mouse pointer, as shown in Figure 0.10.

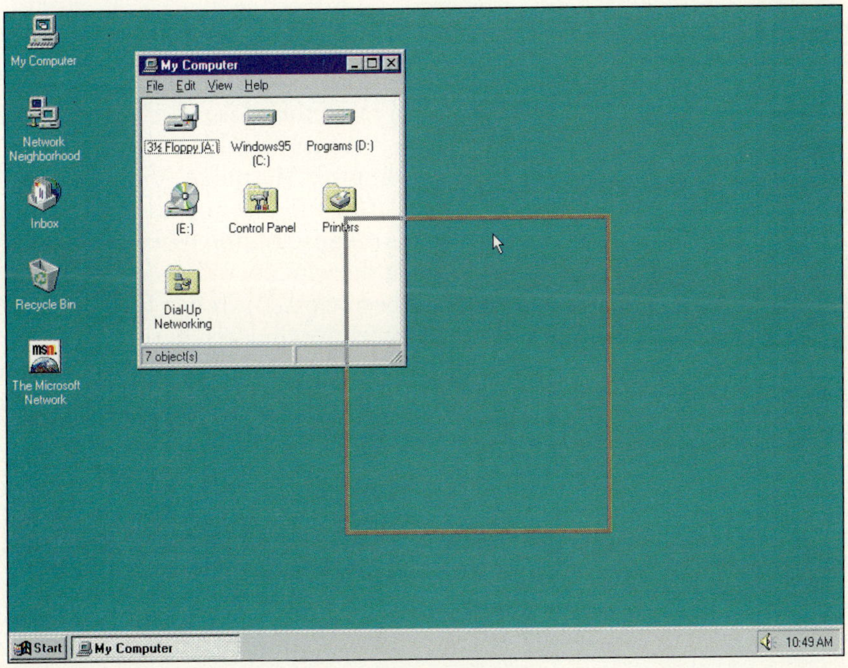

Figure 0.10

3 Release the mouse button.
The window is repositioned wherever you release the button.

Window Buttons

Window buttons perform specific window commands when you select them. These commands are Close, Minimize, Maximize, and Restore. The My Computer window, by default, will display the Minimize, Maximize, and Close window buttons, as shown in Figure 0.11. The Restore window button is available after you maximize a window; it replaces the Maximize button.

Figure 0.11

The Close window button performs the most obvious action. Clicking the Close window button with the mouse closes the window.

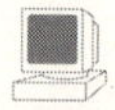

To close a window:

1 Position the pointer over the Close window button on the My Computer window.

2 Click the Close window button.
The window is closed.

The Minimize, Maximize, and Restore window buttons are closely related and are used to change the state of the window you are manipulating. You will recall that it is possible to size the window to your heart's content, in small increments, with the size grip and the borders of a sizable window. The Minimize, Maximize, and Restore window buttons allow you to quickly size a window to preset dimensions.

The Minimize button makes the window disappear from the screen, although the window will retain its Taskbar button. A minimized window has *not* been closed; it is just hidden from view. This can be useful when there are many windows on the screen, and you want to clean things up a bit but keep the various windows readily available. When a window is minimized, you can restore it to its former size and position by selecting its Taskbar button.

To minimize a window:

1 Double-click the My Computer icon to open the My Computer window.

2 Click the Minimize window button.
The window disappears but its Taskbar button remains, as shown in Figure 0.12.

Figure 0.12

3 Click the My Computer Taskbar button to restore the window.

The Maximize window button expands the window to occupy the whole screen (less the space occupied by the Taskbar). When a window is maximized, the Maximize window button is replaced by the Restore window button. Clicking the Restore button will return the window to the size and location it was before it was maximized.

To maximize and restore a window:

1 Click the Maximize window button.
The My Computer now appears maximized. The Maximize window button has been replaced by a Restore window button.

2 Click the Restore window button to restore the My Computer window to its original size and location.

Menu Bar

Many windows will have a ***menu bar*** located directly under the title bar. Menu bars contain ***menu titles,*** which can be selected to access ***pull-down menus.*** These menus contain ***menu items,*** which represent commands that you can select to perform various actions. The My Computer window, shown in Figure 0.13, has a somewhat typical menu bar.

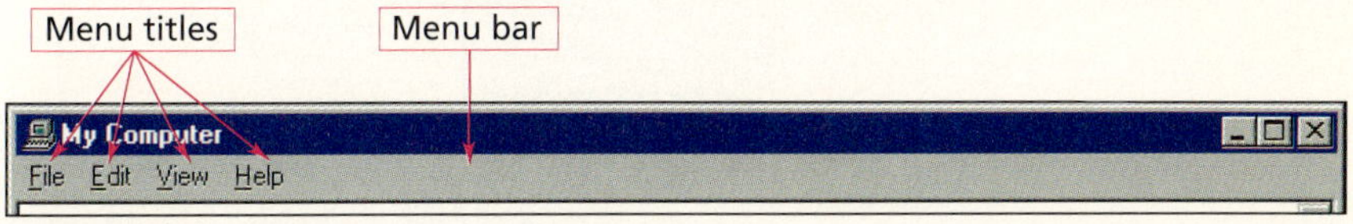

Figure 0.13

When you select a menu title, that menu is displayed and the menu title is highlighted. The menus in Windows will remain open until you select something else.

To select menus in a window:

1 If the My Computer window is not already open, open it now by double-clicking the My Computer icon.

2 Move the mouse pointer to the File menu title, and select the File menu title by clicking it.
The File menu appears as shown in Figure 0.14.

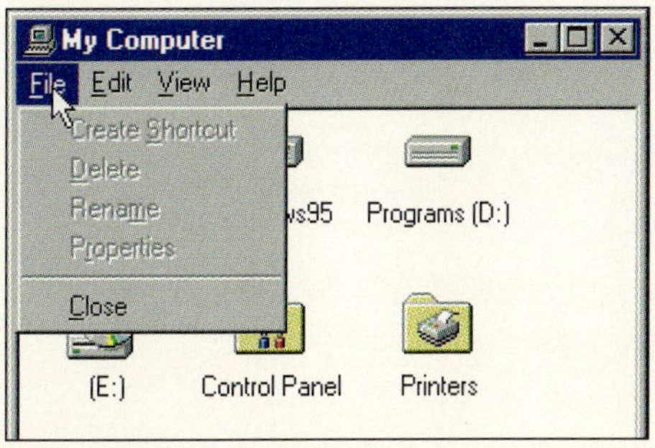

Figure 0.14

3 Release the mouse button, making sure that you do not press any other buttons.
Notice that the menu stays open.

4 Move the pointer slowly over the Edit, View, and Help menu titles, watching as each corresponding menu opens as the pointer moves from menu title to menu title.

5 Move the mouse in a circular motion around the screen.
The menu remains open unless you click something else on the Windows desktop.

6 Move the pointer over the File menu title again.
The File menu opens.

7 Move the pointer slowly down and up the menu, noticing that each menu option is highlighted as you pass the pointer over it.

8 Finally, move the pointer over the Close menu option in the File menu.
The Close option is highlighted, as shown in Figure 0.15.

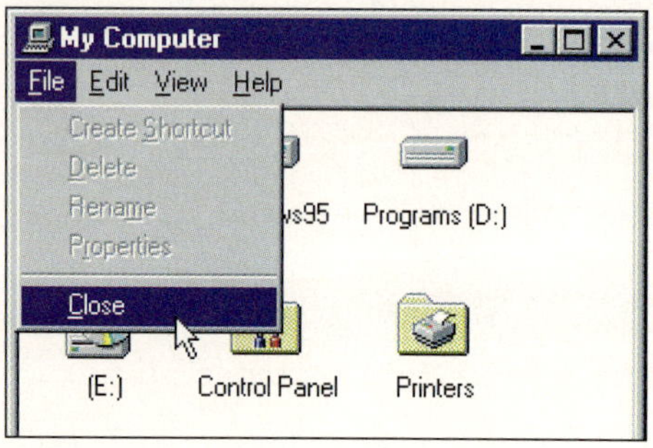

Figure 0.15

9 Select the Close menu option by clicking the left mouse button.
The My Computer window is closed.

Status bar

A ***status bar*** appears at the bottom of a window, although one is not found in each window. It is used to display important information about the window or program. The status bar in the My Computer window, for example, will display the number of objects found in that window, as shown in Figure 0.16.

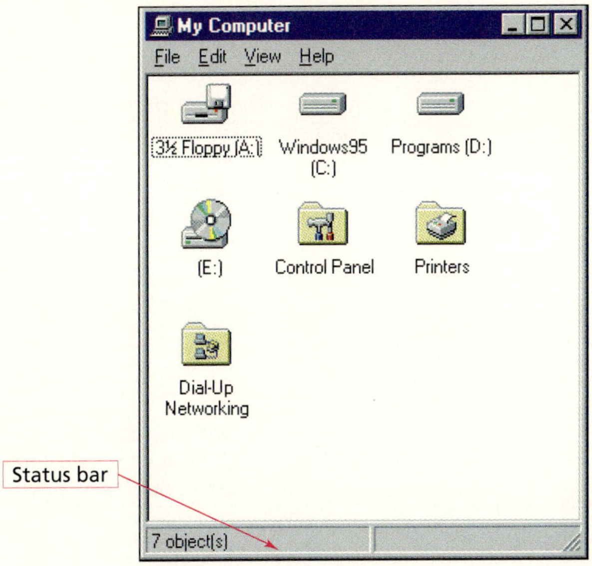

Figure 0.16

When you select an object in the My Computer window, the status bar will change to display information about the currently selected object. For example, if a hard drive is selected, then the status bar displays information about that drive's free space and capacity.

EXIT If necessary, you can exit Windows 95 now and continue this Overview later.

Using Controls

Controls are the means by which you interact with windows. They are graphic objects such as buttons, scroll bars, and text boxes that allow you to perform actions, issue commands, and display information. Generally, each control's appearance is also designed to suggest its use; arrows and buttons are clicked, text boxes invite you to provide input or use the information they display, check boxes toggle functions on and off.

Table 0.1 summarizes the major controls.

Tip Most controls can be disabled; that is, though you might be able to see them on-screen, they cannot be selected or used with the mouse.

Table 0.1

Example [Image]	Name	Description
	Group box, also called frame	***Group boxes*** are used extensively as containers to organize other controls. You can read group box titles to help identify the purpose of a group of controls. Normally, you do not manipulate a group box itself but rather the controls it contains.
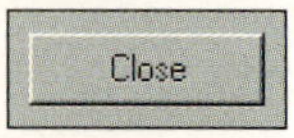	Command button, also called push button	When clicked, a ***command button*** performs some action (usually immediately). Typical command buttons are Open, Close, Cancel, and OK.
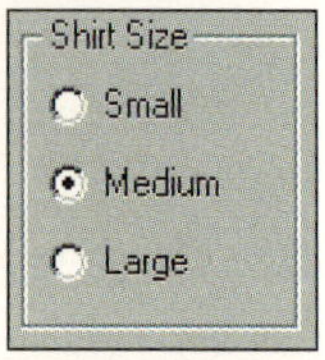	Option button, also called radio button	An ***option button*** can be on or off. In a group of option buttons, the buttons are *mutually exclusive;* that is, only one option can be on at a time.
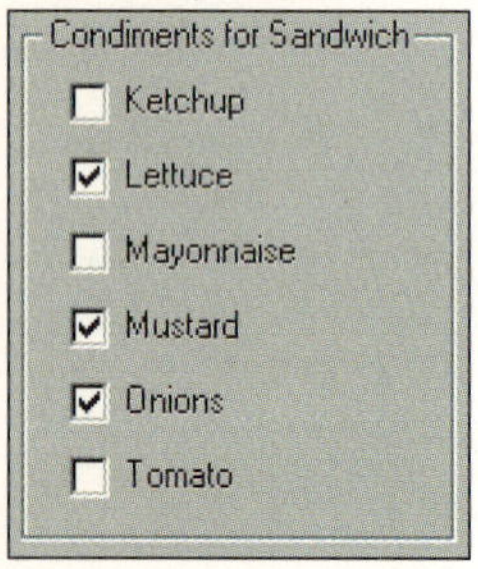	Check box	A ***check box*** can be either on (checked) or off (unchecked). In a group of check boxes, each box can be set independently of the others; that is, any combination of on and off is possible in the group.
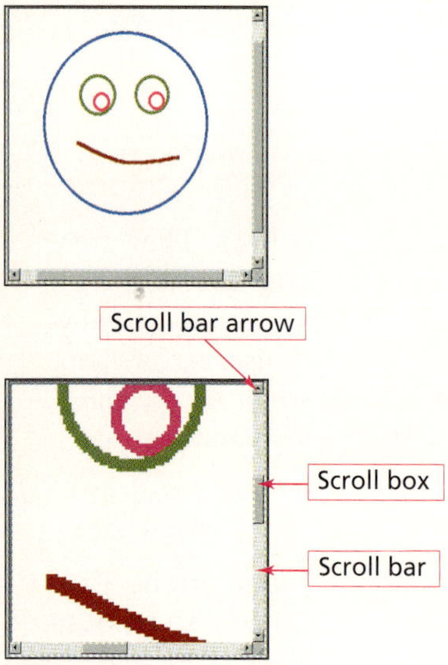	Scroll baryScroll box	A ***scroll bar*** is used to change your view of a document (text, image, list, chart, and so on) that is larger than can be seen in the viewing window. The size of the ***scroll box*** is proportional to the amount of the total image you can see. The larger the scroll box, the more of the complete image is visible. The position of the scroll box indicates the position of the viewing window in relation to the edges of the complete document. The ***scroll bar arrow,*** located at the ends of both scroll bars, moves the window in the smallest increment.
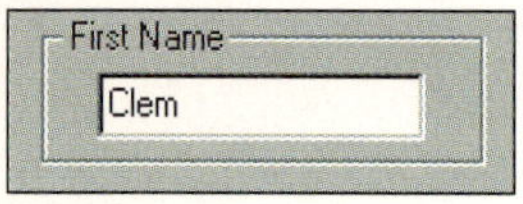	Text box, also called Edit box	***Text boxes*** allow you to type in text of your choice. You can also select and edit text already in a text box.

Example [Image]	Name	Description
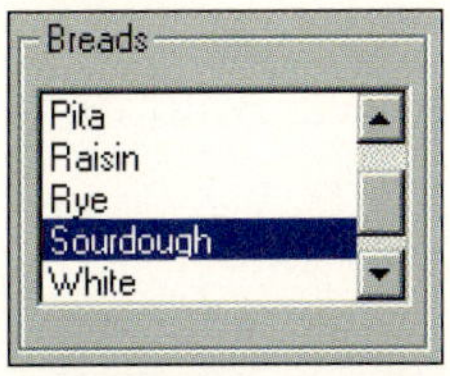	List box	A ***list box*** displays a list of items; you can use the mouse to select one (or sometimes several) of the items. If the list is long, scroll bars are included to allow you to move through the list.
	Combo box	A ***combo box*** combines a text box with a list box. If you don't find what you are looking for in the list, you can type it in at the top of the combo box.
	Spin box, also called spinner	Clicking the arrows to the right of a ***spin box*** causes the value in the box to change (up or down).
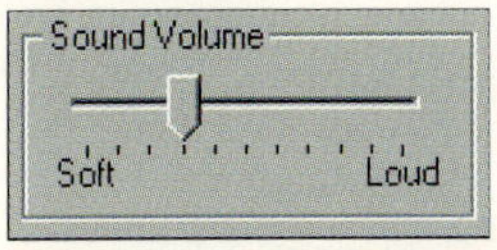	Slider, also called trackbar	***Sliders*** are used to adjust the magnitude of certain settings whose numerical description may not be as easily understood.
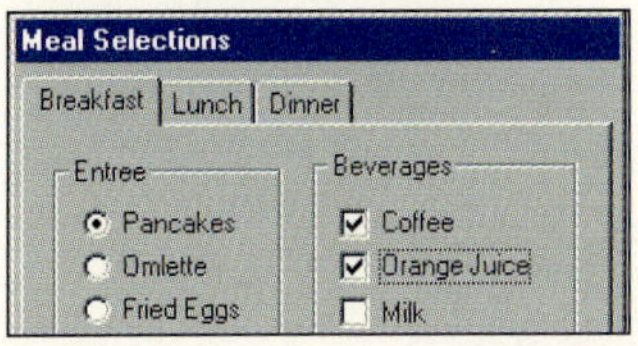	Tab, or tabbed Dialog box, also called notebook tab control or property sheet	***Tabs*** are used to organize different "pages" or panels of controls. Clicking on a tab brings its page into view, where you can then manipulate its controls. Tabs make it possible for menus to be shallower (have a shorter series of choices).

Getting Help in Windows

Windows has an array of tools that provide you various levels of help. One of the biggest complaints with previous versions of Windows was the Help system. If you are making the transition from Windows 3.x, you will be happy to see that the amount and quality of help that now exists has increased dramatically. If you are new to Windows, you will probably wonder what people were talking about when they said that computers were unfriendly!

Context-Sensitive Help

Windows provides context-sensitive help for almost every object on the screen. This help takes several forms, but you are already familiar with the biggest one: the pop-up menu. When you right click an object, a context-sensitive pop-up menu appears.

> ***Reminder*** If you are ever unsure about exactly what you can do with any object, just right click it.

Tooltips

Tooltips, another form of contextual help, are small pop-up windows that appear over a control when the mouse pointer alights over the control for a short period of time. The pop-up window will display a brief text message that describes the control. Typically, tooltips are displayed over controls that have graphic, rather than textual, labels.

The Help Topics Dialog Box

Windows offers extensive help and reference information, right on the computer. The Help system offers excellent search features, and contents and indexing capabilities. Best of all, the same Help interface is used in every Windows program, not just for Windows itself. Once you have learned how to use Help, you do not need to learn a new Help system for every application program too.

The Help system is accessed through the Help Topics dialog box. This can be quickly accessed from the Start button, located in the lower-left corner of the screen.

To open the Help Topics dialog box:

1 Click the Start button.
The Start menu appears.

2 Choose the Help menu item on the Start menu.
The Help Topics dialog box opens as shown in Figure 0.17.

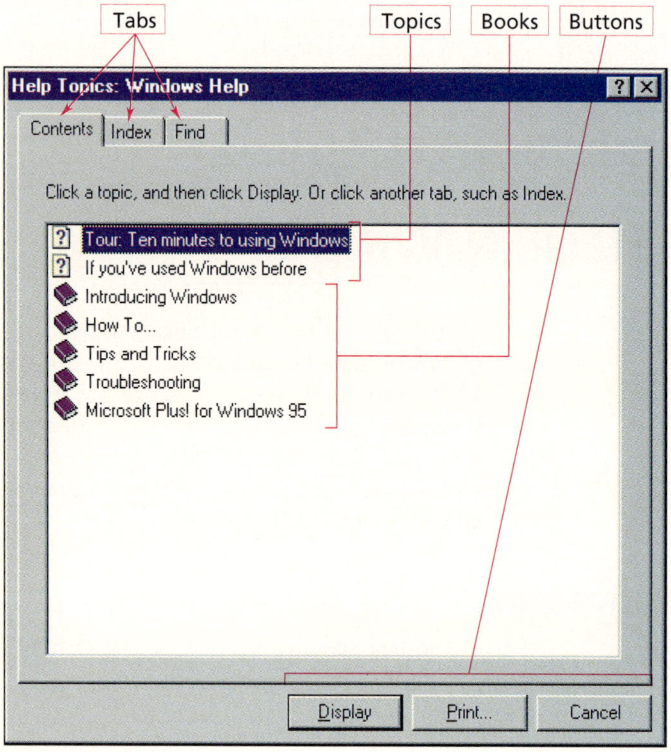

Figure 0.17

The Help Topics dialog box has three tabs, or pages. Like tabs in a notebook, these can be selected, which takes you to the next tab or "turns" the page.

Contents Page

The Contents page, which appears in the front by default, displays a list of *books* and *topics,* organized by category. ***Topics*** are informational files that you can open and read, and ***books,*** like their real-world counterparts, can be opened revealing a list of topics. To view a topic, you can double-click on the topic or its icon, which resembles a little piece of paper with a question mark on it. To open a book, you double-click the book title or its icon.

> ***Tip*** Like most actions in Windows, there is an alternative way to open the books and topics in Help. You can also click a book or topic with the left mouse button and then click the Display button, found at the bottom of the dialog box.

You will now take a look at one of the topics. Since you are new to Windows, you may want to find out something about it. The Introducing Windows book looks like it may hold some relevant information.

To explore the Contents page of Windows Help:

1 Double-click the book labeled *Introducing Windows.*
A new list of books appears.

2 Double-click the book labeled *Getting Your Work Done.*
This displays a list of topics.

3 Double-click the topic labeled *The basics.*
This window offers you the chance to find out about various Windows basics, most of which you learned about in this Overview. You may want to read up on some concepts here or just look around.

4 Move the pointer slowly over the label *Moving windows.*

> ***Tip*** If your Help topics does not include this one, choose another that interests you.

The pointer changes from a small arrow to a little hand that points to the gray box as you pass over it. This is a visual clue that the item you are pointing at is a link and can be accessed with a single click. When you select this item, you will jump to a new page in Help. This type of interface is called hypermedia, and is also the interface for the Internet's most popular service, the World Wide Web.

5 Select *Moving windows.*
The right side of the window displays a small video player that plays a short animation describing how to move windows.

6 Click the Video Play button, located near the bottom of the window. The button resembles the Play button on a CD player or VCR. Now you can watch a short video. A lot of the topics in this section contain short videos like this that describe how to move, scroll, and close windows. Check them out if you are interested.

7 Close the Help window by clicking the Close button, located at the upper right corner of the window.

Index Page

The Index page of the Help Topics dialog box is a list of topics sorted by keyword, much like the index in a book. There is a place to enter a keyword, or you can select a keyword from the list.

Find Page

The third page in the Help Topics dialog box, Find, provides you with full text-search capability. This means that Find will search the Help files for *any* word, using a database that contains *every* relevant word that exists in those Help files (it does not search for words like *the* and *that,* however). Obviously, this is a powerful feature. If you cannot find the help you need in the Contents or Index pages, then the Find page is the place to look.

Find is a little more complex than Contents or Index. Basically, you will enter the word that you are looking for. Help will search its database, looking for words in the database that match the word you entered. It will display a list of these words, which you can choose from. Based on the word (or words) you choose, Find will display a list of Help pages that contain those words.

THE NEXT STEP

This has been a whirlwind introduction to Windows 95. Make sure you re-read any sections that seem unclear to you or access the Windows Help system if you feel that you need more assistance. Project 1 will acquaint you with the various components of the Taskbar and Start menu, explain how to launch application programs, and show you how easy it is to run more than one program at a time.

This concludes the Overview. You can take a break and exit now, or go on to work the Study Questions.

Summary and Exercises

Summary

- Windows 95 is a modern operating system that employs the desktop metaphor and a graphical user interface.
- Overlapping rectangular areas called windows are used to contain separate programs.
- Everything in Windows is an object.
- The mouse is the primary navigational tool for use with Windows.
- Context-sensitive pop-up menus abound in Windows, offering options and properties for the currently selected object.
- Windows can run more than one application program at any given time.
- Windows provides extensive on-line help.
- Windows must be shut down properly before you turn off the computer.

Key Terms and Operations

Key Terms
application program
book
check box
click
combo box
command button
double-click
drag
drop-down menu
frame
graphical user interface (GUI)
group box
icon
left mouse button
list box
menu bar
menu item
menu title
object
operating system
option button
pop-up menu
process
right mouse button
scroll bar
scroll bar arrow
scroll box
shell
size grip
slider
spin box
status bar
tab
text box
title text
tooltips
topic
window

Operations
Click the mouse buttons
Close a window
Display a pop-up menu
Double-click
Get help
Maximize windows
Minimize windows
Move the mouse
Move windows
Restore windows
Select a menu item
Shut down Windows
Size Windows
Start Windows
Use a menu
Use controls

Study Questions

Multiple Choice

1. What does GUI stand for?
   a. general underlying integrator
   b. guaranteed user input
   c. graphics uniform interpreter
   d. graphical user interface
   e. grammatical universal interface

2. Which scroll bar component moves the window in the smallest increment?
   a. scroll bar shaft
   b. thumb
   c. scroll bar arrow
   d. scroll box
   e. None of the above.

3. To open a pop-up menu
   a. click the object with the left mouse button.
   b. click the object with the right mouse button.
   c. double-click the object with the left mouse button.
   d. double-click the object with the right mouse button.
   e. click the pop-up menu toolbar button while the object is selected.

4. Everything in a Window is a(n):
   a. icon.
   b. program.
   c. data fork.
   d. object.
   e. process.

5. When shutting off your computer for the day, which option should you select from the Shut Down Windows dialog box?
   a. Shut down the computer?
   b. Restart the computer?
   c. Restart the computer in MS-DOS mode?
   d. Close all programs and log on as a different user?
   e. None of the above.

Short Answer

1. Windows facilitates multiple programs being run simultaneously, which is called __________.
2. The __________ is used to resize the window.
3. Name the three components of a scroll bar.
4. Name the three tabs of the help window.
5. Name the four types of window buttons.

For Discussion

1. What is the difference between an operating system and an application program?
2. Why do you think a GUI environment like Windows 95 makes running more than one program at a time easier?
3. Describe why the mouse is so important in Windows.

PROJECT 1: GETTING STARTED WITH WINDOWS

Objectives

After completing this project, you should be able to:

- Maneuver through the Start menu
- Use the Start button and Start menu to launch application programs
- Use documents
- Run more than one program at a time
- Switch between windows using the Taskbar

USING THE START BUTTON

In the "good old days" of DOS, users were confronted with an unfriendly C:\> prompt when the system finished loading. Earlier versions of Windows improved the situation somewhat, providing a more pleasing graphical screen, with windows and icons. Unfortunately, Program Manager, the old Windows shell, was not friendly enough: New users were often unsure where they should begin, confronted with an interface that seemed to offer no help. The Start button in Windows 95 remedies this situation, providing an obvious place to begin your exploration of Windows.

Opening the Start Menu

To start Windows and open the Start menu:

1 If you have not already done so, turn on the computer system. Windows will load.

2 If necessary, log on to Windows using your user name and password.

3 Close any open windows.

4 Click the Start button.
The Start menu opens as shown in Figure 1.1.

Figure 1.1

Touring the Start Menu

The Start menu is called a ***cascading menu*** because its submenus cascade, or flow off of, the main menu. The Start menu has several hierarchies of menus, logically categorized. The menu items on the main Start Menu are Programs, Documents, Settings, Find, Help, Run, and Shut Down. To the right of some items on the Start menu are right arrows. These arrows indicate that submenus open when you select those items. Now you will take a look at the Start menu and its major features.

The Programs Menu Item

The Programs menu item cascades to reveal a menu of application and accessory programs. Programs is at the top of the main Start menu for a reason: When running Windows, you are doing so to use application programs like Word and Excel. The Programs menu contains both *program items* and *program group items.* The ***program items,*** which may include the MS-DOS prompt and Explorer as well as other application programs installed on your system, are denoted by miniature application program icons. The programs are executable, meaning that selecting the icons will cause that program to run. ***Program group items,*** like Accessories, are system tools that are indicated on the Programs menu by a special program group icon. When you select this icon, further menus are revealed. For example, when you select the ***Accessories*** program group icon, you will see a menu of the small programs that are included with Windows. These programs include a paint program, a calculator, a word processor, and others.

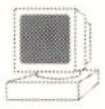

To display submenus on the Start menu:

1 Move the pointer over the Programs menu item, being careful not to press a mouse button.
After a brief pause, a new menu opens as shown in Figure 1.2.

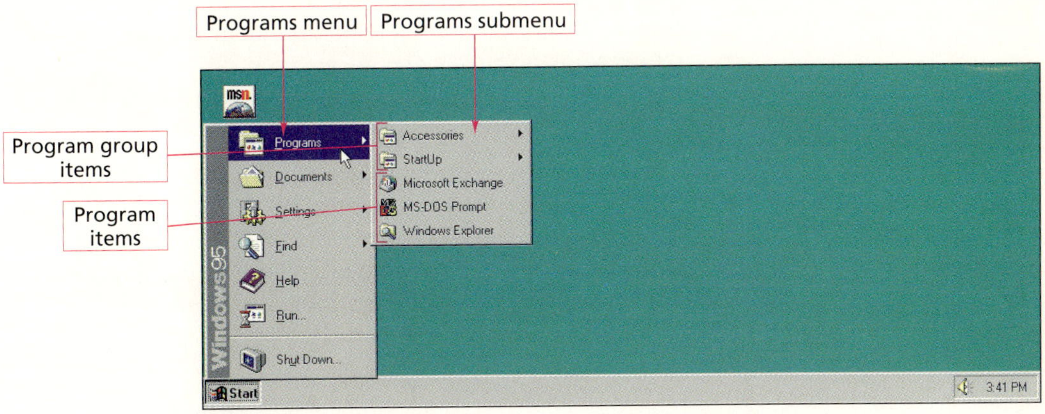

Figure 1.2

2 Move the pointer over the Accessories program group. The Accessories menu cascades open as shown in Figure 1.3.

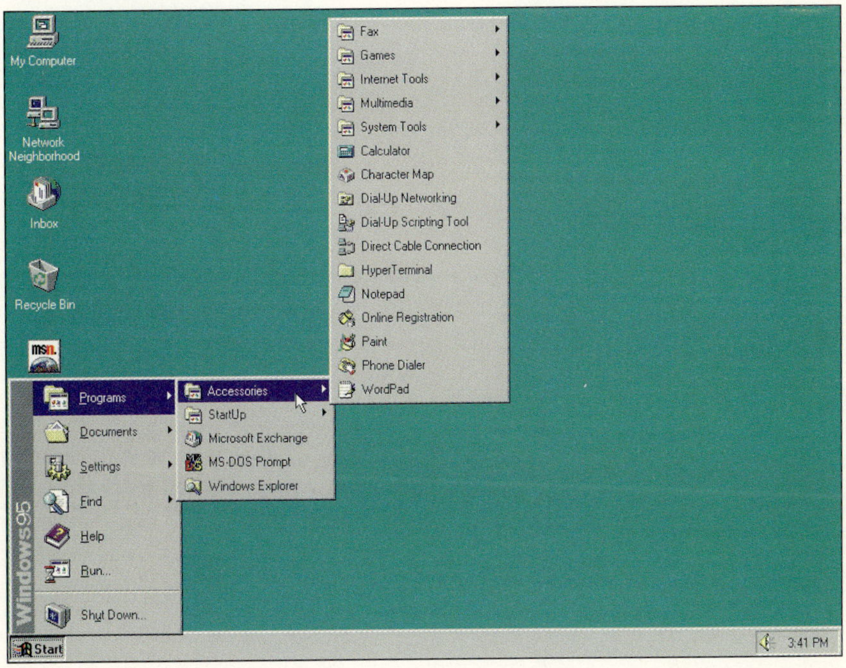

Figure 1.3

Reminder The program and program group items on your screen may be slightly different than the ones shown in the figure. Each site will have different software installations, and the Start menu will accordingly be different to reflect what software is available.

You can close each succeeding cascading menu by selecting items on previous menus. To close all menus but the main Start menu, move the pointer over to one of the items on the main Start menu that does not cascade, such as Find or Help. The menu should collapse, or close, and return to its original state.

The Documents Menu Item

The Documents menu displays a list of the last 15 documents you accessed. If, for example, you write a letter in a word processing document, save it, and then close the word processor, that letter will appear as an item in the Documents menu. This provides you with a quick way to return to the documents you have been working on recently.

The Settings Menu Item

The *Settings* menu items allow you to change the Windows configuration options, configure the Start menu, and set up your printer.

The Find Menu Item

Windows offers a powerful search utility program called Find, which can be accessed most easily from the Find menu item. You can use Find to find files or folders on your computer, find computers on a network, or find files or folders on other computers on a network.

The Help Menu Item

Help is easily accessible through the Start menu. Refer to the Overview if you need a refresher on using Help.

The Run Menu Item

The Run menu item allows you to run a Windows or DOS program quickly by typing its name and pressing ENTER Typically, it is used to execute infrequently accessed programs that are not represented in the Start menu.

The Shut Down Menu Item

As described in the Overview, the Shut Down menu item brings up a dialog box with various Windows shut-down and restart options.

EXIT If necessary, you can exit Windows 95 now and continue this project later.

WORKING WITH APPLICATION PROGRAMS

Windows is pretty interesting in and of itself, but the big question is "What can you do with it?" Operating systems exist to provide an environment for application programs to run in. There are more application programs available for Windows than for any other operating system, and Windows 95 can also run programs written for MS-DOS and older versions of Windows.

You have looked at the Start menu but have not used it for its primary purpose: starting application programs. If you want to write a letter, for example, you will need to start a word processor. You have also looked quickly at the powerful Find utility, but what happens when you find the file you were looking for? Why were you looking for that file in the first place? Most likely, you wanted to open it. If it is a bitmap graphic file, then you probably want to open it into a paint program so you can edit or print it out.

Launching Programs

Programs can be ***launched,*** or started (sometimes referred to as executed or run) in many ways. Here, we will discuss the most direct way: through the Start menu. The Start menu is, as you recall, a doorway to the application programs that exist on your computer. Cascading menus lead you through program groups that contain program items. The program items on the Start menu are shortcuts, or links, to programs that exist somewhere on the hard drive of the computer. Using the Start menu does not require you to understand where these programs reside, although you will be learning about that in upcoming projects. All you need to do is find the program item you want, select it to launch the program, and then use the program.

To launch a program from the Start menu:

1. Restart Windows, if necessary.
2. Open the Start menu.
3. Move the pointer to the Programs program group item.
   The Programs submenu cascades open.
4. Move the pointer to the Accessories program group item.
   The Accessories submenu cascades open.
5. Move the pointer to the Paint menu item, as shown in Figure 1.4.

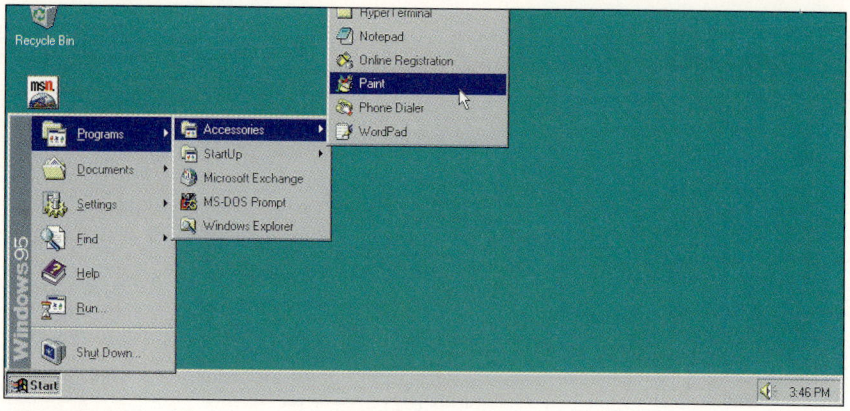

Figure 1.4

6 Select the Paint program item to launch the Paint program. The screen should now resemble Figure 1.5. If the Paint window appears maximized, you can click the Restore window button to make it a smaller window.

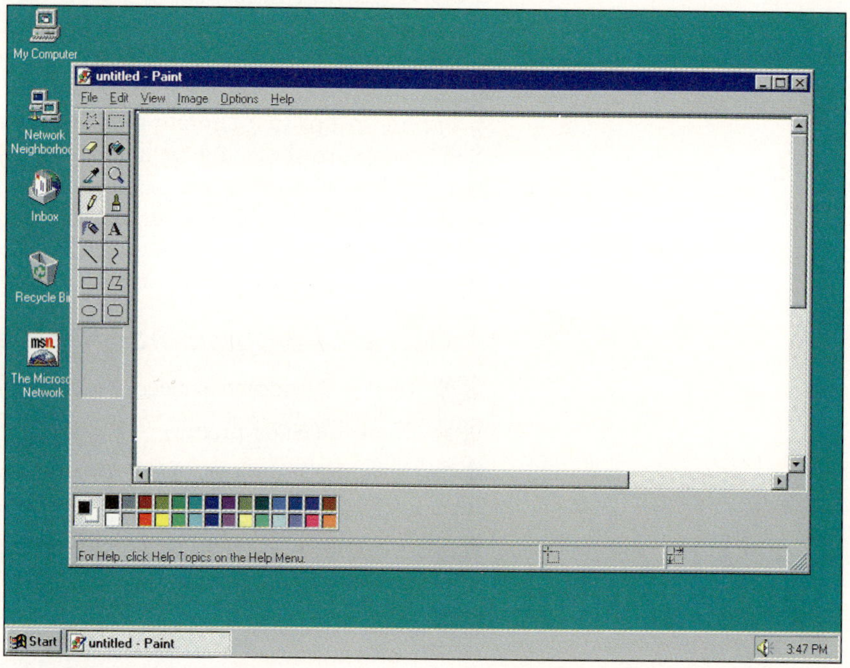

Figure 1.5

Paint, like most Windows applications, runs in a resizable window. It has an application icon, a title bar, and window buttons. It also has a ***toolbox,*** running along the left side of the window, as well as a color palette. A toolbox is a collection of icons that gives you quick access to commonly needed tools similar to the toolbars that many application programs use.

Any time a window is opened, a corresponding button is placed on the Taskbar. Opening Paint places a button on the Taskbar that has a title identical to the title on the Paint window, in this case *untitled—Paint.*

Using Documents

Application programs are the tools that you use to create *documents.* A ***document*** is any kind of data file—a letter, image, or other file that is created by an application program. Paint has loaded with the caption *untitled-Paint* in the title bar. There is no document name in the title yet because the document that is loaded into Paint right now is blank, or empty. Most application programs will start with an empty document. This allows you to get to work right away, without having to create the empty document first.

There are several operations involving documents. You can choose, for example, to save the current document or open a previously saved document. For now, you will open a Paint document, which is known as a *bitmap* file.

To open a bitmap file:

1 Select File from the menu bar.

2 Select the Open menu option, as shown in Figure 1.6.
The Open dialog box appears showing the folders and bitmap files in the Windows folder.

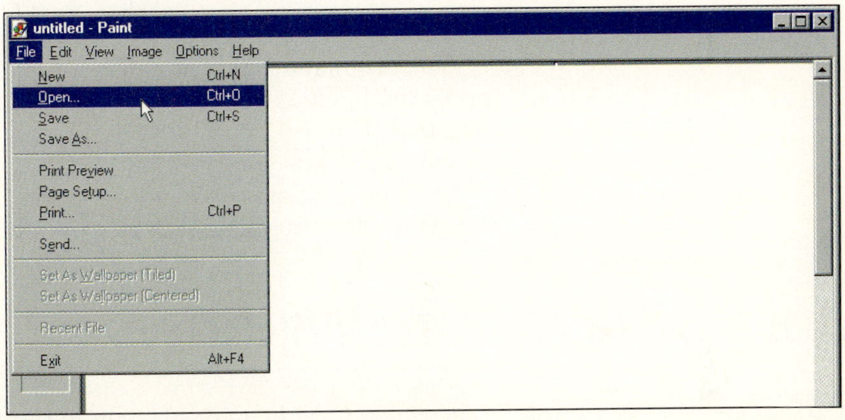

Figure 1.6

The screen will now resemble Figure 1.7.

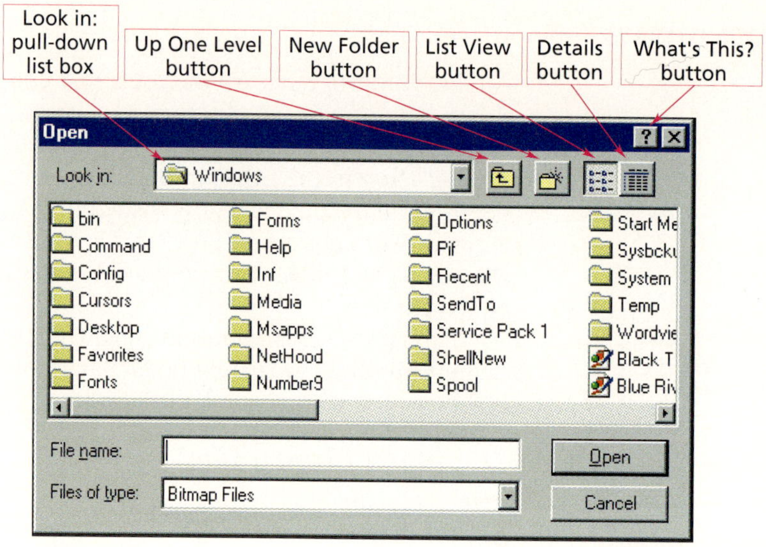

Figure 1.7

3 Select one of the bitmap files and then click the Open button. The bitmap file is now loaded into Paint.

You may want to play around with Paint for a few minutes—it is a fun program. It allows you to create 256-color graphical images and has a surprisingly broad range of tools, given the fact that it comes free with Windows. When you are done painting, you will take a look at how application programs in Windows can coexist with each other. Make sure you leave Paint running, though; you will be using it in the next section.

Multitasking with Windows

The ability of an operating system to run more than one program at a time is called ***multitasking.*** Windows supports multitasking handily—you can have dozens of programs running in Windows with little loss in speed, especially if your computer has a lot of memory. The usefulness of multitasking is something that is hard to understand until you have experienced it. You may think that you would never want to run more than one program at a time, but once you start using this feature, you will find it hard to believe that there was a time when such a thing was impossible. Like most features in Windows, multitasking is handled in a straightforward way. You will now launch a second program to demonstrate some simple multitasking techniques.

To launch another application program:

1 Make sure that Paint is still running.
If it isn't, follow the steps in the previous section to launch Paint again.

2 Open the Start menu, select the Programs group item, and then select Accessories.

3 Select WordPad.
WordPad is a word processor that is provided free with Windows. After a brief pause while the program loads, the WordPad window appears as shown in Figure 1.8.

Figure 1.8

When two or more windows are open, you can choose which window is the current, or selected, window by selecting the title bar of the program you wish to bring to the foreground.

> ***Tip*** You could actually select any area of a program's window to bring it to the foreground. It is safest to select the title bar, however, because you could cause an unintended action to occur if you select an area of the window that contains controls or data.

To switch between running programs:

1 Use the mouse skills you developed in the Overview to resize and drag the Paint and WordPad windows as necessary so the screen resembles Figure 1.9. Make sure that WordPad is in the foreground by selecting its title bar.

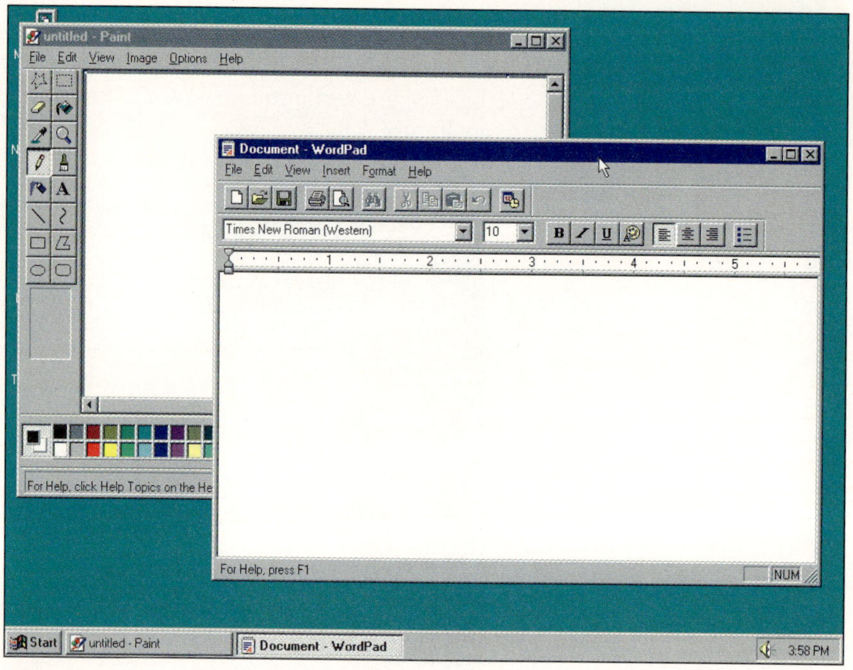

Figure 1.9

2 Select the Paint title bar.
The WordPad title bar becomes gray, indicating that it is no longer the current window. Paint's title bar, meanwhile, becomes blue, and the entire Paint window springs to the foreground and overlaps WordPad. This effect is shown in Figure 1.10.

Figure 1.10

3 Select the WordPad title bar to bring it to the front again.

Reminder This module uses the default Windows screen colors. If your setup has been modified, the colors may be different.

Using the Taskbar to Switch Between Programs

The method of selecting each program's title bar works fine if you can get at the title bars, but what happens when a window is maximized and you want to reach another window that is completely hidden beneath the maximized window? An inelegant solution would be to minimize the maximized application and then restore it when you were done with the other window. While this would work, there is a better way. You will recall that the Taskbar displays a button for each window that is open. This includes windows that are open but minimized. Selecting a window's Taskbar button will bring that window to the front and make it the currently selected window.

To use the Taskbar to switch between programs:

1 Click the Maximize window button to maximize the WordPad window. Now the Paint window is hidden, although Paint is still running.

2 Click Paint's Taskbar button, as shown in Figure 1.11.

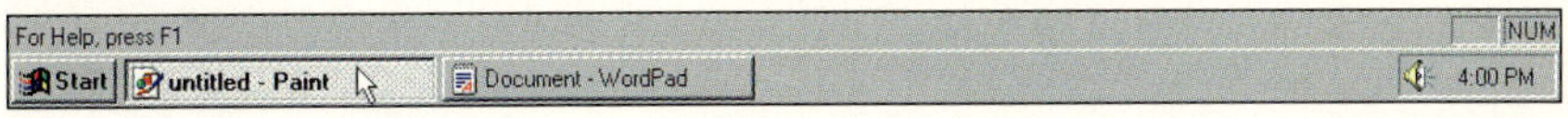

Figure 1.11

Paint now jumps to the front.

3 Click WordPad's Taskbar button.
WordPad, once again, is the current window.

4 Close the WordPad and Paint windows and any other windows that may still be open.

You will find the Taskbar very convenient as you use Windows. Many application programs are run maximized, and the Taskbar gives you an easy way to switch from window to window, similar to the way that a channel-changer on a television set can switch from one TV station to another. You know that a television program on one channel is still being shown even if you are watching something else. You can verify this by changing channels if you wish. The Taskbar accesses running programs in a similar manner.

THE NEXT STEP

Windows is a powerful operating system that can exist on a stand-alone computer or on a network. It supports a variety of controls that make interacting with the operating system easy, and it lets you run multiple programs at the same time. This multitasking is made easier with the Taskbar, which allows you to switch among all running programs. In the next project you will begin your exploration of file management. Managing files is important on any computer, and My Computer offers a simple yet powerful interface for this task.

This concludes Project 1. You can either shut down Windows now or go on to work the Study Questions, Review Exercises, and Assignments.

Summary and Exercises

Summary

- The Start menu is a logical place to start exploring Windows. You open the Start menu by double-clicking the Start button, located in the lower-left corner of the screen.
- The Start menu is a cascading menu featuring quick links to application programs and system tools.
- Find is a powerful utility program that can locate files and folders on the computer's drives.
- Documents are data files created by application programs.
- Windows can multitask, or run more than one program at a time.
- You can switch between running programs with the Taskbar.

Key Terms and Operations

Key Terms
accessories
cascading menu
document
file extension
launch
multitasking
program items
program group items
toolbox

Operations
Find files
Launch application programs with the Start menu
Multitasking with the Taskbar
Navigate the Start menu
Open a document file
Run more than one program at a time

Study Questions

Multiple Choice

1. Most application programs load with
   a. the last document opened.
   b. an empty document.
   c. a blank screen.
   d. a pretitled document.
   e. a graphic.

2. How do you get from one window to a hidden window?
   a. Minimize the window in the foreground.
   b. Reopen the application from Programs.
   c. Use the Find menu.
   d. Use the button on the taskbar.
   e. None of the above.

3. Multitasking means
   a. connecting two or more computers in parallel.
   b. connecting two or more computers in serial.
   c. connecting two or more computers to a single printer.
   d. connecting two or more printers to a single computer.
   e. running two or more programs on the same computer simultaneously.

4. *Launching* a program means to
   a. copy the program to a hard disk
   b. load a program into main memory and execute (run) it.
   c. save a data file from an application to any type of disk storage.
   d. install a program to a hard disk.
   e. exit (close) a program window.

5. What file type is commonly used to identify Windows graphics?
   a. ISO
   b. bitmap (BMP)
   c. ANSI
   d. color map
   e. palette file (WPF)

Short Answer

1. What items will you find on the Start menu?
2. How do you collapse a menu?
3. __________ are data files created by application programs.
4. How do you switch between running programs?
5. Running more than one program at a time is called __________.

For Discussion

1. What is the most direct way to launch a program? What is one way to open a document? Why are they different?
2. Why is multitasking such an important feature of Windows?

Review Exercise

Using the Start Menu

Different corporate and educational sites running Windows 95 will have varying contents for the Start menu. You should acquaint yourself with what is available on the system you use.

Begin by clicking on the Start menu and noting each of the options that initially appear. Then proceed to examine any menu items that have submenus. Get a sense of how things are organized on your particular system—what the major branches and subbranches of the Start menu contain. Practice "backing out" of submenus with the mouse. For the Programs submenu, write down a list of the items available (including the submenus within Programs).

Assignment

Multitasking and Window Manipulation

Use the Start menu to launch the following three accessory programs: Calculator, Paint, and WordPad. Maximize each program's window. Practice using the Taskbar buttons to switch among the three programs. Finally, practice resizing, moving, and minimizing each program's window. When you are finished, close each of the programs.

PROJECT 2: FILE MANAGEMENT WITH MY COMPUTER AND EXPLORER

Objectives

After completing this project, you should be able to:

- Use My Computer and Explorer to browse through the resources on your computer
- Recognize and use folders and files
- Create, copy, move, rename, and delete files
- Use Cut, Copy, and Paste with files

MANAGING FILES WITH MY COMPUTER

The hard drive on the computer you are using is filled with thousands of ***files.*** Don't worry, that's not a bad thing—the files on the computer make up the Windows operating system, the application programs you use, and the documents you create. A file is nothing more than a collection of ***bytes,*** small units of information storage that are magnetically smeared across the surface of a disk or etched with a laser onto the underside of a CD-ROM.

Windows offers several methods of dealing with files. In this project you will be exploring the simplest file-management tool: My Computer. You will recall that the My Computer object, an icon sitting on the Windows desktop, is intended to be the obvious place to go when you want to look at the files and resources on your computer.

My Computer is a browser and file manager. This means that it is used to examine and manipulate the files that exist on your computer's disk drives. It also supplies a front end, or interface, to various system resources like configuration options, printers, and Dial-Up Networking.

Tip Dial-Up Networking is not installed on every Windows system.

TAKING A CLOSER LOOK AT MY COMPUTER

It's time to take a closer look at the My Computer window and examine its various components. This section focuses on the objects that are specific to My Computer.

To open the My Computer window:

1 Start Windows if you have have not already done so, and log on to the network if required.

2 Insert a blank formatted diskette in drive A: if you have not already done so.

3 Double-click My Computer.
The My Computer window opens as shown in Figure 2.1

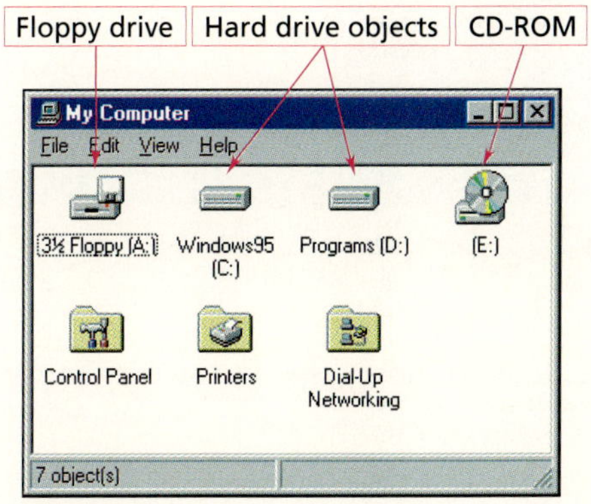

Figure 2.1

Reminder The My Computer window on your system may differ slightly, depending on the hardware and software that is installed. Some computers will have two or more floppy drives, or only one hard drive. Some may not have a CD-ROM drive. You may also not see a Dial-Up Networking folder. Don't worry, the basics will be the same.

The My Computer window consists of various objects that represent physical and logical locations in your computer. Physical locations include all types of drives: floppy, hard, CD-ROM, and others. The logical locations are represented by icons that look similar to file folders. These special folders represent system resources, such as printers and system configuration tools.

The File System

The computer's file system consists of at least one hard drive, usually C:, and at least one floppy drive, usually A:. The C: drive is the boot, or start-up, drive, and it is from here that the system will load when you start the computer. Back when DOS was king, you would be confronted with a C:\> prompt when the system finished booting and would then have to type obtuse commands to navigate through the file system. Today, Windows boots to a graphical interface, and to navigate through the file system, all you need is a mouse. For starters you will take a look at the file system on the C: drive.

To look at the file system on drive C:

1 Double-click the C: drive icon.
A new window opens as shown in Figure 2.2

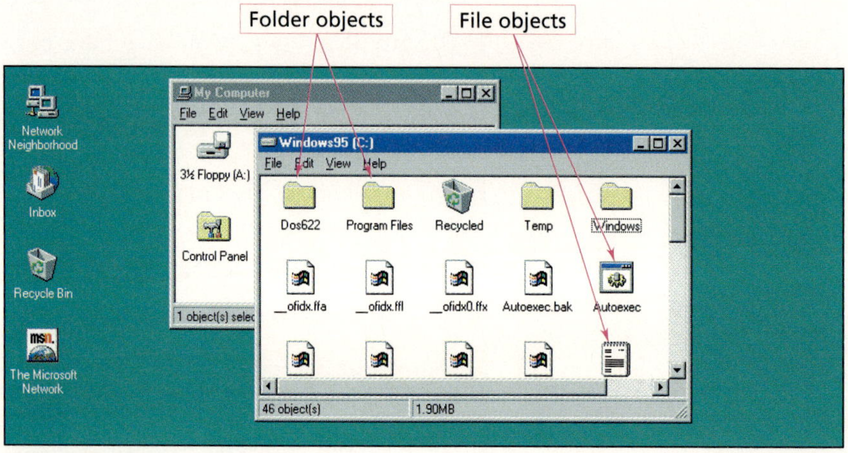

Figure 2.2

The new window displays the contents of drive C:.

Files and Folders

The C: drive contains files and *folders*. ***Folders*** are objects that contain files and possibly other folders. When the IBM PC first came out, there was no way to store files in folders; files on any given disk (usually a low-capacity floppy disk) all had to be in the single root directory of the disk. As advancements in storage capacity and the proliferation of files made this method unreasonable, the ability was added to allow folders, or directories as they were then called, to exist on a disk. This made it possible to arrange files logically on a disk so you could, for example, have separate directories for your DOS files, word processing program files, and data files. Today, computer file systems are made up of many nested folder levels, with folders inside of folders inside of folders.

You may have heard the term ***tree*** used to describe a directory structure. In many ways a directory structure *is* like a tree, but the tree is upside down. As shown in Figure 2.3, a simple directory structure would have the ***root,*** or ***parent,*** folder at the top. The root can have files in it (like startup files that need to be there when the system boots), and folders, like Windows and Temp. These folders can then have files and other folders inside of them (and they do—the Windows directory contains hundreds of files in dozens of directories!).

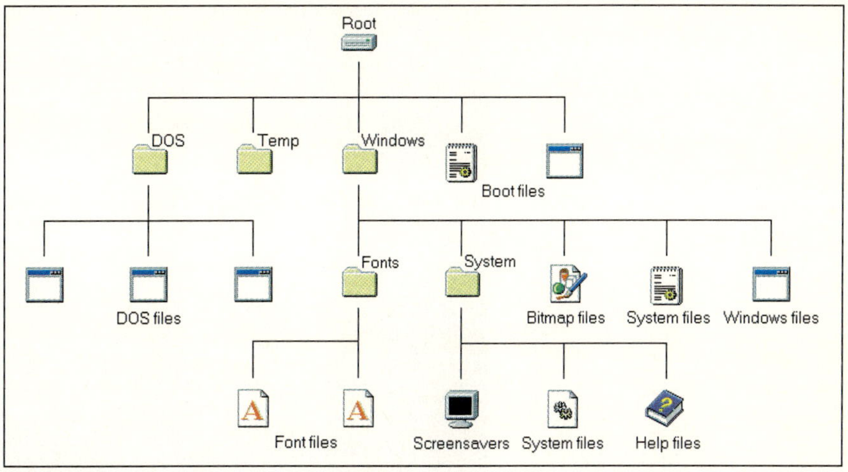

Figure 2.3

Opening Folders

Every time you open a drive object in My Computer, a new window opens, displaying the name of the drive in its title bar to let you know what you are looking at. You are also confronted with a list of folders and files that are contained within that drive. Opening a folder will likewise display the contents of that folder.

To open a folder in My Computer:

1 If it is not already open, double-click the drive C: icon in My Computer.

2 Double-click the folder called Windows.

A new window opens as shown in Figure 2.4.

> ***Tip*** *Windows* is the default name for the directory where the Windows files are stored. It is possible, however, for this directory to have another name, like Win or Win95.

Notice that folders are displayed first, in alphabetical order. Then files are displayed, also alphabetically. Notice also that a Taskbar button is created for every window you open from My Computer, allowing you to easily navigate among these windows. Figure 2.4 shows the three Taskbar buttons and windows that you should see.

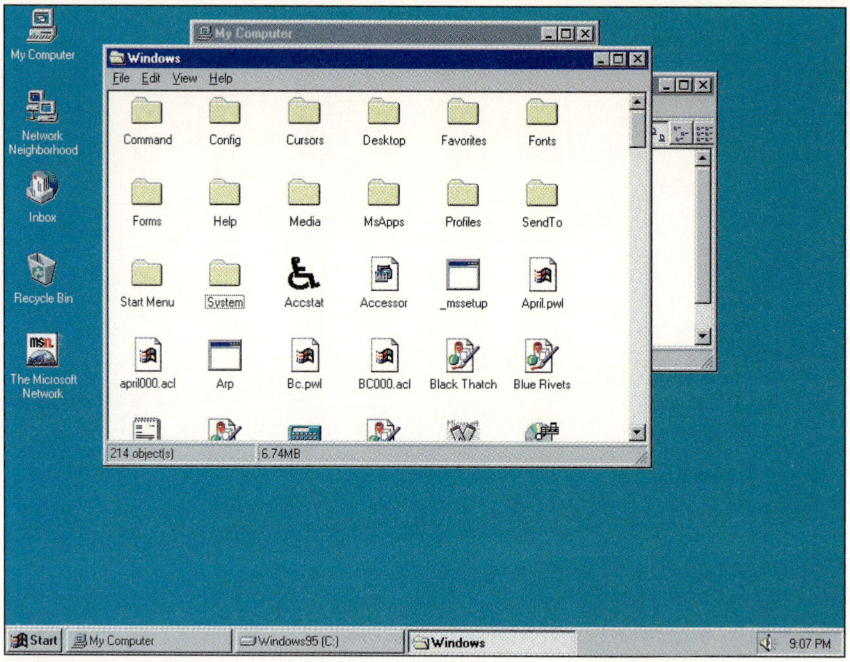

Figure 2.4

Running Programs from My Computer

You can also execute programs from My Computer by double-clicking that program or its icon. You will try this out with a program called Notepad, which is a simple text editor that comes with Windows.

To run a program from My Computer:

1 Use the scroll bars to scroll through the Windows folder until you find the Notepad program icon.

2 Double-click the Notepad icon.
The Notepad program opens. As you would expect, a new Taskbar button for Notepad is created as well.

3 Click the Close button to close Notepad.
Alternatively, you could choose Exit from the File menu.

Navigating Through Multiple Windows

Now you have got a number of windows open, and the screen is starting to get a bit cluttered. My Computer is consistent in the way that *something* happens every time you double-click an object. If you double-click a program file, that file executes. If the file is a document, then that document is loaded into an application program that is able to display it. If a folder is double-clicked, a new window opens.

This type of reaction from the system is great because it gives you feedback on your actions. The problem is, how do you deal with all those windows on the screen if you have been opening folder after folder? It is possible to have dozens of open windows on the screen.

Unfortunately, there is no easy answer. Some people like the way My Computer does things. Others, especially those who enjoyed using the File

Manager in Windows 3.1, will probably like using Explorer more than My Computer. Explorer performs the same functions as My Computer using a slightly different interface. The differences between Explorer and My Computer are described later in this project.

EXIT If necessary, you can exit Windows 95 now and continue this project later.

MANIPULATING FILES AND FOLDERS

Browsing through the file system, opening and closing files, is all very nice, but you need to have a reason for doing so. The types of operations that you can do with files and folders is extensive, but the most common are creating, copying, moving, renaming, and deleting.

Creating Files

You can create document files in Windows with application programs, but you can also create certain types of files without opening an application at all. The types of files you can create this way are determined by the software installed on your computer. With only Windows installed, you should be able to create, at the very least, text files, bitmap files, and WAV (music and sound) files. Now you will create an empty text file on your diskette.

To create a blank text file:

1 Reopen Windows if necessary.

2 Insert a work diskette if necessary, and bring the My Computer window to the foreground.

3 Double-click the drive A: icon.
A window opens, displaying the folders and files on the diskette.

> ***Tip*** If the diskette in drive A: is not formatted (prepared for use), Windows will allow you to format it now. Go ahead and do so, and then continue with these steps.

4 Right-click an empty spot in the A: window.
A pop-up menu for drive A: appears as shown in Figure 2.5.

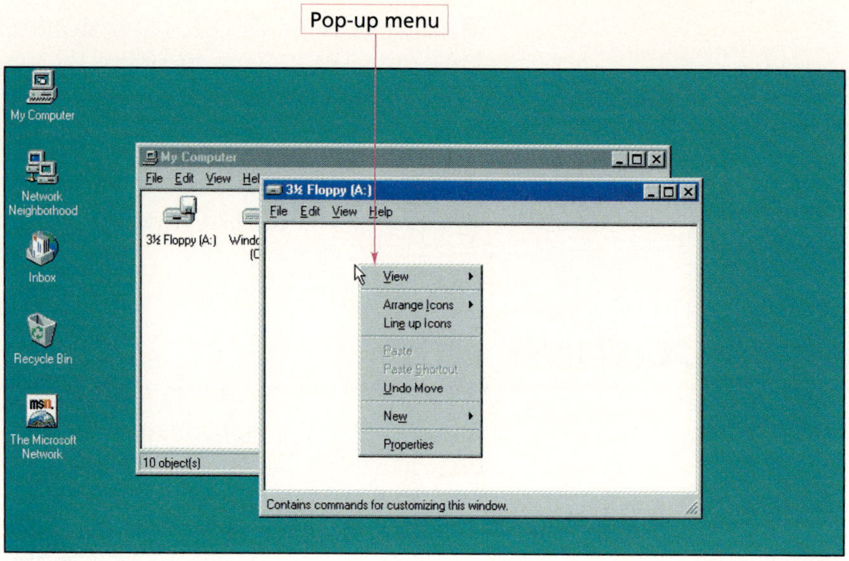

Figure 2.5

5 Select the New menu item.
A submenu cascades open. (You could also just move the pointer over the New menu item and wait a moment. The submenu will appear after a brief pause.)

6 Select Text Document.

7 A new text file appears in the drive A: window, with the highlighted title New Text Document, as shown in Figure 2.6.

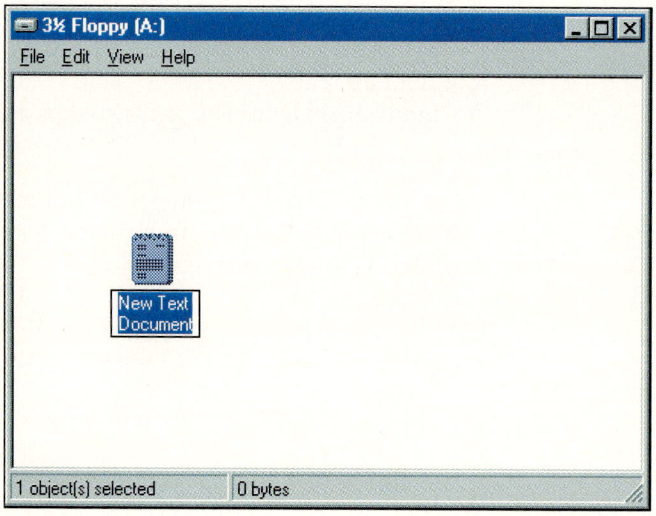

Figure 2.6

When a title is highlighted, you can change the title by simply typing a new one.

8 Type `My first text file` and press (ENTER)
The name of the file you have created is *My first text file.* The file itself is empty, meaning that it contains no text.

You have created a new text file without having to open Notepad or some other text editor. To launch Notepad, you could now double-click on this file.

Creating Folders

You can create new folders in a similar manner. In fact, you will find that the creation of folders is a far more common occurrence than creating blank document files.

To create a new folder:

1 As before, select a blank area of the drive A: window and right-click.
A pop-up menu opens.

2 Select New and then Folder.
A new folder appears, with the highlighted caption *New Folder*.

3 Type `My first folder` and press ENTER to name the new folder.
As you can see, folder creation is a relatively simple procedure.

> ***Reminder*** Folders are not files, they are containers that can hold files and other folders. Think of a folder as being equivalent to a desk drawer or actual file folder: they are all used to store documents.

Copying Files and Folders

You have created a new folder and a new file. Now what? You can *copy* your text file into the new folder. ***Copying*** a file means that you are creating a duplicate of that file in another location. The end result is that you will have two identical files with the same name in different places. When you back up a hard drive, for example, you are making a copy of the files on that hard drive and placing them in another place where, you hope, they will be safe.

The copy operations for files and folders are virtually identical. Remember that copying a folder will copy *all* of that folder's contents. This means that copying a folder full of other folders and files will make a duplicate copy of all of those items as well.

One way of copying a file entails performing an operation called ***drag and drop,*** which is one of the most common Windows operations. When using drag and drop, you select an object with the mouse and move, or drag, it across the desktop to its new location, which could be on another drive or another computer completely if you are on a network.

Objects have default operations when dragged and dropped using the left mouse button. It is better to use the right button, however, which displays a pop-up menu for each drag and drop, giving options for operations.

> ***Caution*** It is not a good idea to rely on default drag and drop operations. If you are unsure what the drag and drop is going to do, use the right mouse button. That way you cannot accidentally move a file, effectively deleting it from its original location.

To copy a file using My Computer:

1 Right-click the icon for the new text document, *My first text file,* but **do not** let go of the mouse button.
When done properly, no pop-up menu appears.

2 Drag the file icon to the icon for the new folder, *My first folder,* while holding down the right mouse button.

3 When you have reached the folder, release the mouse button.
A pop-menu appears as shown in Figure 2.7.

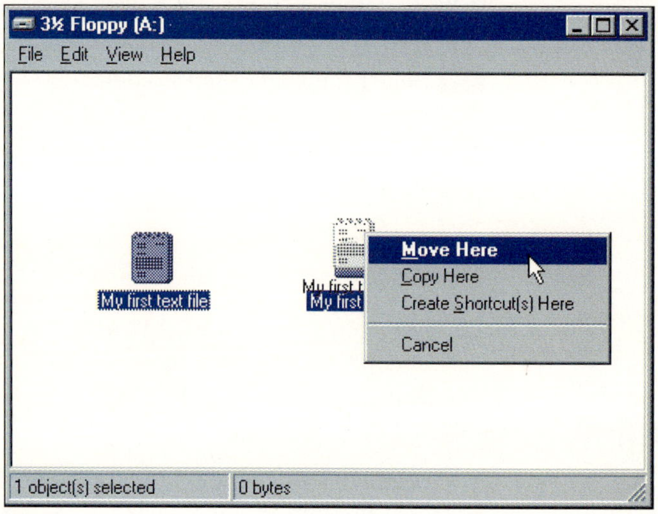

Figure 2.7

4 Select Copy Here.
The disk drive grinds away for a second, and then the window returns to the way it was before you copied the file. Notice that the original text file you created is still sitting there, as before.

5 Open the folder labeled *My first folder.*
A new window opens and displays the duplicate copy of the text file that you made, as shown in Figure 2.8.

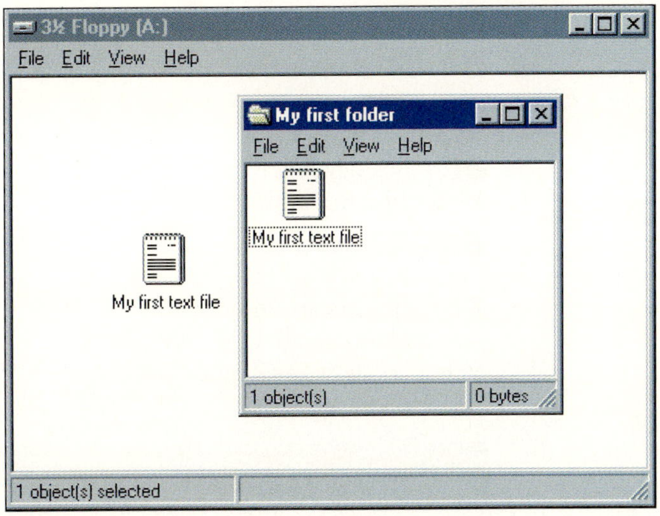

Figure 2.8

6 Close the *My first folder* window.

Moving Files and Folders

What if you want to "pick up" a file and *move* it to a new location (and not just create a duplicate)? In other words, you want to move the file from one place to another. This action is called, appropriately enough, ***move.*** The move operation is also very similar for files and folders. Remember that moving a folder moves all of its contents as well.

As you did with copying, you will move a file by performing a drag and drop operation with the right mouse button. The only real difference between copy and move is that you will choose the Move option when the drag is complete. You will begin by creating a new file to move.

To move a file:

1 Right-click a blank area in the drive A: window.
A pop-up menu appears.

2 Select New and Bitmap Image.

3 Name the new image *My first bitmap.*

4 Right-click *My first bitmap,* drag it to *My first folder,* and then release the mouse button.
A pop-up menu appears.

5 Select Move Here.
Your file disappears.

6 Open *My first folder* to see that your *My first bitmap* file has indeed been moved.

Renaming Files and Folders

When you create a new file or folder, you are given the chance to name it when it is created. You may want to rename the file later, though. This is easily accomplished using the ***rename*** operation, and the action is exactly the same for both files and folders. In this example, you will rename the new bitmap file you just created and moved.

To rename a file:

1 Click *My first bitmap.*
It becomes highlighted, showing that it is selected.

2 Wait a moment and then click it again, making sure that you select the label and not the icon.
A box appears around the object's label, and the label is highlighted. The pointer has changed into an insertion point, meaning that text can be edited, as shown in Figure 2.9.

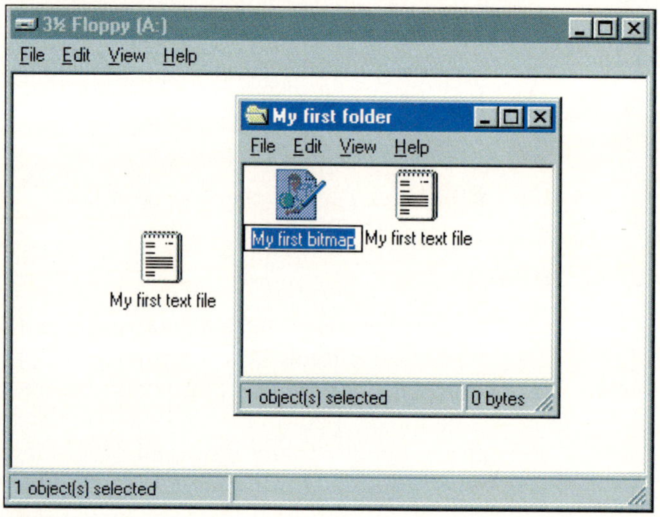

Figure 2.9

3 Type `I renamed this bitmap!` as the new title, and then press (ENTER)
The bitmap has been renamed. That's all there is to it.

> ***Tip*** If you select the title too quickly, the system will read your two clicks as a double-click and will open the file you are trying to rename. In the case of your bitmap file, Windows will launch Paint. If this happens, close Paint and try again—this time making sure to time your clicks a little farther apart.

Deleting Files and Folders

There comes a time for every file or folder when it has outlived its usefulness. The demonstration files and folder you have been working with were fun for a while, but their services are no longer required. You will now delete them. Deleting a file sounds rather ominous, but in fact deleted files and folders can be recovered later under certain conditions.

When you delete Windows files, they are placed in a special folder called the Recycle Bin. The Recycle Bin is represented on the Windows desktop by the Recycle Bin icon. It works like a real recycle bin: When you delete a file or folder, it is placed in the Recycle Bin (which is really just a folder) so you can reuse it later. To physically remove the file from the hard drive forever, you must empty the Recycle Bin.

You will now delete the newly created text document and folder (which has two files in it). You could delete them separately, but Windows supports a handy extended-selection feature that will allow you to delete both objects at once.

To delete files and folders with My Computer:

1 If it is still open, close the window *My first folder*.
The drive A: window remains open and is in the foreground.

2 Drag the pointer across the window, creating a rectangular region that covers the *My first folder* and *My first text file* objects, as shown in Figure 2.10.

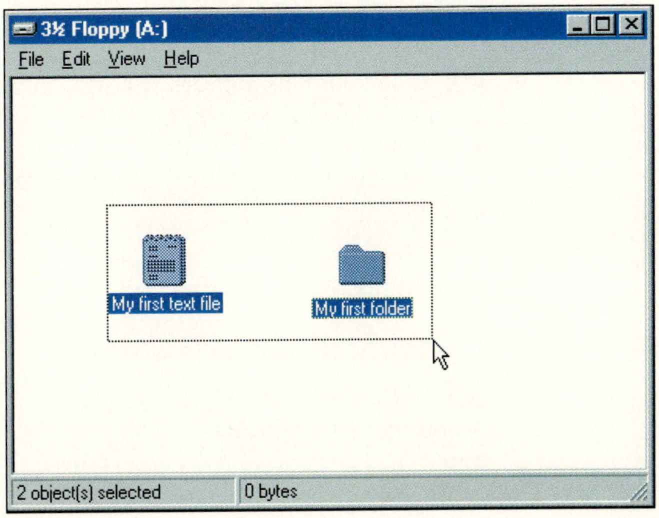

Figure 2.10

Make sure you do not select any other objects.

> ***Tip*** You can also select multiple objects with CTRL To do this, select the first object normally. Then hold down CTRL and select each additional object.

3 Release the mouse button and position the mouse pointer over either of the selected icons.

4 Holding the mouse button down, drag the two files to the Recycle Bin icon on the desktop, as shown in Figure 2.11.

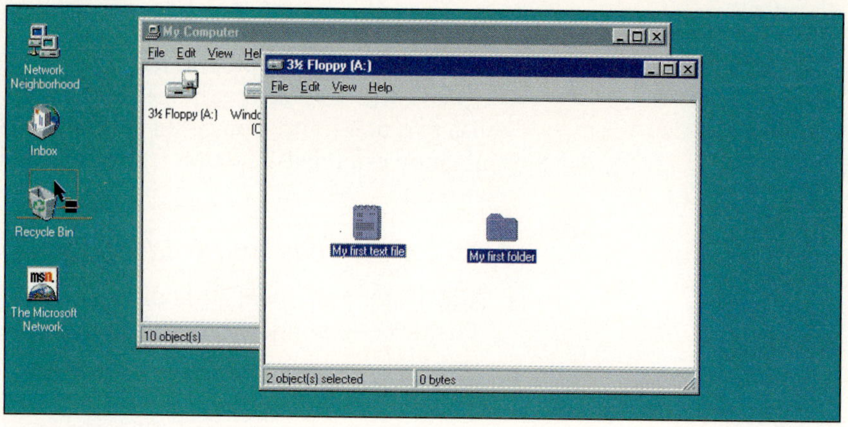

Figure 2.11

5 Release the mouse button.

6 If a dialog box appears, asking you if you are sure you want to delete the files, click the yes button.
The icon for the Recycle Bin changes from an empty looking bin to one that is full of papers. This is a visual indication that the files have been deleted.

To remove these files from the hard drive for good, you must empty the Recycle Bin.

To empty the Recycle Bin:

1 Right-click the Recycle Bin object.
A pop-up menu appears.

2 Select the option titled *Empty Recycle Bin.*
A dialog box will appear, asking you if you are sure that you want to delete the files. You are.

3 Click the Yes button.
The files are now removed for good.

4 While you are cleaning up, close any other windows that may be open, using the skills you have developed thus far.

Using Cut, Copy, and Paste with Files

As you become more acquainted with various application programs, you will find that you frequently use the operations Cut, Copy, and Paste. These operations are similar to the Move, Copy, and Delete operations you looked at earlier. In the past Cut, Copy, and Paste were used in application programs like word processors to manipulate text. Today they are integrated right into Windows and are used to manipulate files and folders as well. You can access Cut, Copy, and Paste most easily by right-clicking the object you want to manipulate and then selecting the appropriate options in the resulting pop-up menu.

Tip You can also access the Cut, Copy, and Paste operations from the Edit menu of almost any window.

Cut and Paste

The Cut operation is used in conjunction with Paste to move a file or folder. You will recall that moving a file or folder means that you delete it from its original location and transfer it to a new location. It is analogous to grabbing any object you may find around the house and putting it someplace else. The object still exists, but it is in a different place.

> ***Reminder*** Multiple selections are possible as well when performing Cut and Paste, or Copy and Paste, operations. You can select more than one file and/or folder and perform these same operations.

To Cut and Paste a file from My Computer:

1 Double-click the My Computer icon.
The My Computer window opens.

2 Double-click the A: drive.
A new window opens.

3 Create a new text file called CutNPaste using the skills you developed in the previous section.

4 Right-click CutNPaste and select the Cut option from the pop-up menu that appears.
The CutNPaste file icon dims somewhat, indicating that it is ready to be moved.

5 Create a new folder named Temp and double-click on it to open the folder.
A window opens, displaying Temp folder.

6 Right-click a blank area of the Temp window.
A pop-up window appears.

7 Select Paste.
The CutNPaste file is moved into the Temp folder.

8 Close the Temp window.
You can no longer see the CutNPaste file in the window that displays the contents of the Text folder, because it is now in the Temp folder.

9 Close the drive A: and My Computer windows.

Copy and Paste

Copy and Paste are used together when you want to make a duplicate of a file or folder, but want to leave the original where it was. The operations are the same as those used in the Cut and Paste example above, with the only difference being that you select Copy instead of Cut.

As you can see, there are a wealth of file-browsing and management options in Windows. For users in a network environment, the same concept of browsing extends to the network as well.

Using Windows Explorer

My Computer provides a basic way to browse the file system and perform file management. Advanced users appreciate a more streamlined interface than My Computer, though, and some people may not like the way My Computer opens a new window every time they double-click a folder or drive object. Windows addresses these issues with an advanced browser and file manager called Windows Explorer, or simply Explorer. Explorer is everything that My Computer is and more, and it offers an advanced interface with which to navigate through the resources on the computer.

The Explorer program allows you to perform any file-management duties, run programs, and open documents, all from a single dual-paned window. This window, shown in Figure 2.12, is split in half vertically. The left half, or ***All Folders pane,*** displays drive and folder icon objects and the right pane, called the ***Contents pane,*** shows the files and folders in the current drive or folder. Opening a folder or drive in Explorer will *not* cause a new window to open, although it will cause the view in the Contents pane to change.

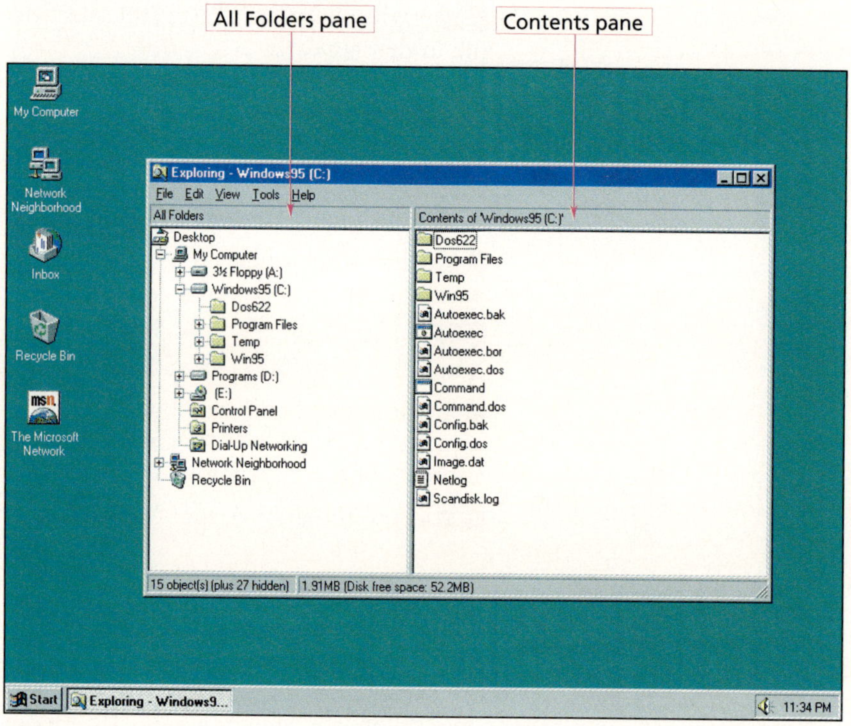

Figure 2.12

Launching Windows Explorer

Explorer, like many programs in Windows, can be launched in several ways. By default, Explorer appears in the Programs group of the Start menu.

To launch Explorer:

1 Click the Start button.
The Start menu appears.

2 Move the pointer over the Programs item.
A submenu opens, as shown in Figure 2.13.

3 Click the Windows Explorer item to launch Explorer.

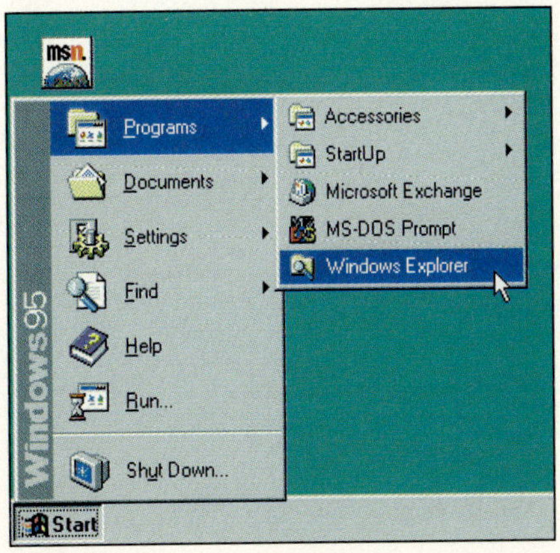

Figure 2.13

Navigating with a Dual-pane Window

The All Folders pane, also known as the Tree pane, is a collapsing "tree" view of the entire system. Each branch on this tree can be expanded and collapsed as you desire, making the view of the file system very adjustable. By default, the Explorer will display its view of your system from the desktop on down, through each of the drives and the resources that make up your computer. This tree view resembles an outline: The indenting style emphasizes the hierarchical nature of the data you are viewing. A file system is inherently hierarchical, with folders inside of folders, and the outline-style tree view offers a logical way to view this data.

Notice the lines and the boxes with plus and minus signs in them in the All Folders pane. The lines indicate the hierarchical relationship between objects. An Expand button (a small box with a plus sign in it) indicates that the object it is next to can be expanded to show more detail. You will see this button next to drive and folder objects. If a drive or folder object is already expanded, the button will change to a Collapse button (a small box with a minus sign in it), indicating that the object can be "closed" to hide the details of its contents. The Expand and Collapse buttons are shown in Figure 2.14.

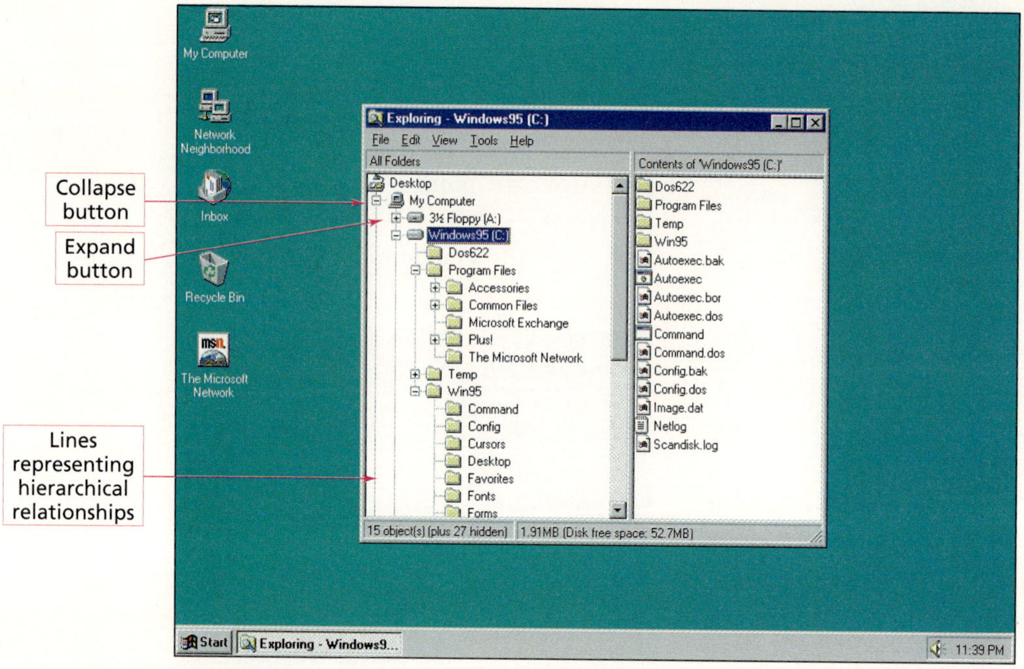

Figure 2.14

Expand and Collapse Buttons

You can use the Expand and Collapse buttons to change the view on the All Folders pane of the Explorer window. The view in the Contents pane will not be affected.

Clicking an Expand or Collapse button affects only the branch that you are working with and will not change the properties of other levels in the tree. Likewise, expanding and collapsing will not change the view in the Contents pane.

Opening a Drive or Folder

The Contents pane can only show one folder's worth of data at a time, so using the Expand and Collapse buttons allows you to navigate to the exact place you would like to view without having to display each subsequent branch in the Contents pane. At some point, though, you will want to see the details in the Contents pane; you can do this by clicking the icon in the All Folders pane that represents the object whose contents you would like to view.

Drives and folders can be opened by clicking their icons in the All Folders pane or by double-clicking them in the Contents pane.

To display the contents of a drive or folder in the Contents pane, you can single-click that object's icon in the All Folders pane or double-click the icon if it is in the Contents pane.

CHANGING VIEW STYLES FOR FOLDER CONTENTS

You can easily change the way items are arranged in the Explorer window. By default, Explorer uses ***List view,*** which automatically sorts the files and folders by type and then alphabetically within each type group. Folders are displayed first and then the files.

There are three other view types, *Large Icons, Small Icons,* and *Details.* ***Large Icons view,*** which is the default view in My Computer, displays the objects as icons. ***Small Icons view*** displays the objects as smaller icons—the same icons that you would see in a window's title bar, in fact. *Large Icons* and *Small Icons* views sort the files alphabetically without regard to type. Folders, as always, are displayed before files. The fourth style, ***Details view,*** adds information about each object's type and the date it was last modified. Details view allows you to sort the objects in various ways as well.

The View menu has items for each of the view styles, and these can be chosen to determine your view preference. The current view style will be marked with a bullet. Alternatively, you can select the view style using the view buttons in the toolbar, located under the menu in the Explorer window. The view buttons are shown in Figure 2.15.

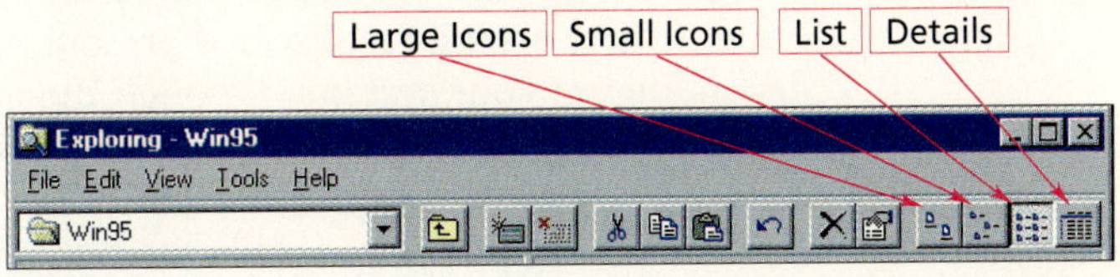

Figure 2.15

Tip If the toolbar is not visible, you can activate it by choosing Toolbar from the View menu.

Tip The View style options discussed in this project are also available in My Computer.

USING THE EXPLORER TOOLBAR

The Explorer toolbar, shown in Figure 2.16, offers one-click access to many of Explorer's options. Earlier you looked at the view style buttons. Clicking a button on a toolbar is faster than searching for that option in a menu. You will now take a look at the other buttons and the Go to a Different Folder drop-down list box on the Explorer toolbar.

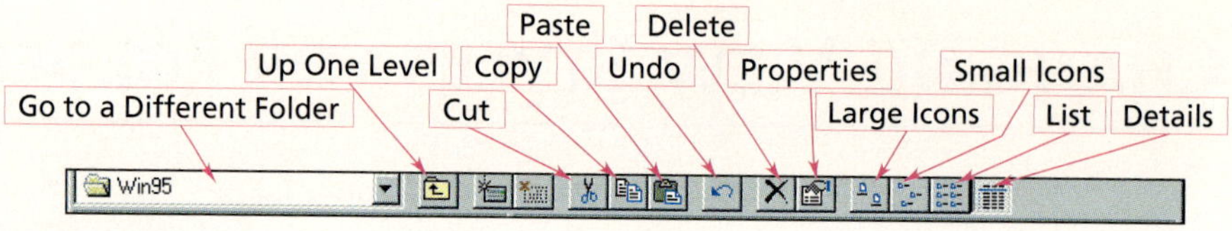

Figure 2.16

Tip If you have trouble remembering which button is which, the Explorer toolbar items have tooltips that will remind you.

Toolbar Items

The Explorer toolbar is a logically arranged collection of buttons, and one drop-down list box situated at the left end of the toolbar. In this section you will explore the various components of the toolbar.

Go to a Different Folder List Box

The leftmost item in the Explorer toolbar is the Go to a Different Folder drop-down list box. This item allows you to choose the resource you want to explore. Resources include the desktop, disk drives, system configuration options, networking resources if present, the Recycle Bin, and other items, depending on your system. To open the drop-down list box, you can click anywhere within its frame or directly on the down arrow located on the right side of the list box.

You may wonder why such a list box exists, when all of the information that it displays is available in the All Folders pane. There are several reasons, but the most important is this: Selecting resources from the drop-down list box will not affect the hierarchical structure of the tree view in the All Folders pane. Jumping from resource to resource with the list box allows you to change the Contents pane without affecting the All Folders pane. This will become important when you begin using Explorer for file management and want to retain the tree view but need to navigate to a different drive.

The Up One Level Button

As you know, Windows organizes objects in a hierarchical structure. It will often be preferable, as you navigate from folder to folder, to return to a folder you have been to previously. In the following steps you will look at the Up One Level button, which allows you to change the focus of the Contents pane to the folder directly above the one you are in currently.

Network Drive Buttons

There are two network buttons in Explorer, Map Network Drive and Disconnect Network Drive. They are used for advanced networking functions and will not be discussed in this module.

Cut, Copy, and Paste Buttons

The Cut, Copy, and Paste buttons on the toolbar work like their menu counterparts: First you select an object that you would like to move (cut) or copy, and then you click the Cut or Copy button. Next you navigate to the location you would like to place the file, display that location in the Contents pane, and click the Paste button.

The Undo Button

The Undo button is used to reverse the last operation you performed in Explorer. This will work for operations like Cut and Paste, Copy and Paste, and Delete. In the previous section you copied a file into the Temp folder on the student data diskette. If you had done this action in error, you could reverse it by pressing Undo.

The Delete Button

The Delete button, located just to the right of Undo, is used to remove objects in Explorer. It works as you would expect: You select the object or objects you want to delete and press the button.

Large Icons, Small Icons, List, and Detail Buttons

The view buttons were discussed in an earlier section of this project. If you need to review their use, you may reread it now.

THE NEXT STEP

My Computer and Explorer offer similar ways to browse through the resources on your computer where files, folders, and other resources are all readily accessible. They are also file managers and offer a wealth of file-management operations, such as Create, Copy, Move (Cut), Rename, and Delete. You can run programs from My Computer and Explorer, and double-clicking a document icon will cause the application program that created that document to load.

This concludes Project 2. You can either shut down Windows now or go on to work the Study Questions, Review Exercise, and Assignments.

SUMMARY AND EXERCISES

Summary

- My Computer and Explorer are resource browsers and file managers.
- A computer's file system will generally consist of at least one floppy drive and one hard drive.
- These drives can contain files and folders. Folders are objects that can contain other files and folders.
- Programs can be run from within My Computer or Explorer by double-clicking the program name or its associated icon.
- Opening a document in My Computer or Explorer will cause the application program that created that document to run, with that document loaded.

- There are several common file and folder operations, including Create, Copy, Move (or Cut), Rename, and Delete.
- Copying and Moving files can involve the common drag and drop operation.

Key Terms and Operations

Key Terms
all folders pane
byte
contents pane
copy
details view
drag and drop
file
folder
large icons view
list view
move
parent
rename
root
small icons view
tree

Operations
Browse through a file system
Change view styles
Collapse & expand the tree
Copy files and folders
Create files and folders
Delete files and folders
Drag objects
Go up one level
Manage files
Move files and folders
Navigate with multiple windows
Open documents with My Computer
Open folders
Rename files and folders
Run programs with My Computer
Use copy and paste with files and folders
Use cut and paste with files and folders

Study Questions

Multiple Choice

1. My Computer and Explorer windows contain all of the following except
   a. hard drive icon(s).
   b. floppy drive icons(s).
   c. a printer folder.
   d. a formatting folder.
   e. folders for system resources.

2. When the computer starts, which drive is normally the boot, or start-up, drive?
   a. B
   b. A
   c. C
   d. the CD-ROM drive
   e. none of the above

3. Folders can contain
   a. files only.
   b. Program Manager groups only.
   c. any object.
   d. files and other folders.
   e. other folders only.

4. What happens if you open a document in My Computer or Explorer?
   a. The document is executed.
   b. A pop-up menu appears.
   c. The document is placed in the Recycle Bin.
   d. Documents cannot be opened in My Computer.
   e. The document is opened using a program that can manipulate it.

5. Which operation would you use if you wanted to make a duplicate of a file, but leave the original where it was?
   a. Cut
   b. Copy
   c. Paste
   d. Move
   e. Create

Short Answer

1. What objects are considered physical locations in My Computer or Explorer?
2. Why is a directory structure sometimes called a tree?
3. How do you run a program from My Computer?
4. How do you create a new folder?
5. Will copying a file result in the original being changed in any way?
6. Why should you drag and drop objects using the right mouse button?
7. Will renaming a file generate a second copy of that file?
8. What file operation would you use to erase a file?
9. Cut and Paste is the same as what other operation?
10. What two operations could be used to make a duplicate of a file or folder?

For Discussion

1. The ability to create folders revolutionized file management on the PC. Why was this so important?
2. My Computer will open a new window every time the user double-clicks a drive or folder icon. How could this create a problem?
3. Describe what happens when you open a folder using Explorer. How is it different from opening a folder using My Computer?

Review Exercise

Examining the File System

Use My Computer to examine the root folders of your computer's local hard drive(s). If the computer is part of a network, take a look at the network drives as well. Get some practice resizing, moving, and closing the many windows that will be created during this exercise. Draw a tree that shows how information is organized on your system and network; make note of the major folders in the root directories, and look for other folders within these. You do not have to list the thousands of individual files!

Assignments

Dragging and Dropping Files and Folders

In this assignment you will use My Computer to "juggle" files and folders. This will provide extensive practice with window management and using the mouse for drag and drop operations.

On a blank disk, create two folders called Reports and Text. In the Text folder, create another folder called Work. Open the Reports folder, and create three new text documents called Rain Forest, Desert, and Coral Reef. Using drag and drop, move the Reports folder (which will include the files you just created) to the Text folder of the diskette. Select the two files Rain Forest and Coral Reef and, again using drag and drop, copy them to the Work folder. Rename the file Desert to Tundra. Finally, delete the Reports folder (which will also delete the files it contains).

Using Cut-and-Paste

This assignment resembles the preceding one, but you will use cut and paste operations. Using Explorer, create folders called Work and Text if they do not already exist.

Open the Work folder. Create a folder within it called Accounts. Open the Accounts folder, and create three new text documents called Payroll, Receivables, and Payables. Using cut and paste, move the Accounts folder (which will include the files you just created) to the Text folder of the diskette. Select the file Payroll and, again using cut and paste, copy it to the Work folder. Rename the Receivables file to Income Statement. Finally, delete the Accounts folder (which will in turn delete the files it contains).

Operations Reference

Menu Item	Icon	Explanation
Programs		Displays a list of programs installed on your computer.
Documents		Displays a list of previously opened documents.
Settings		Displays a list of system components that have settings you can change.
Find		Displays dialog box in which you can specify a folder, file, shared computer or mail message you want to find.
Help		Launches Windows '95 Help feature which gives instructions about how to execute Windows '95 tasks.
Run		Lets you use MS-DOS commands to start a program or open a folder.
Shut Down		Shuts down, restarts, or logs you off your computer.

Operation	Button	Action
Selecting a window		Click once in the window's title bar, or click that window's Taskbar button.
Selecting an icon		Click once on the icon.
Deselecting an icon		Click once on a blank portion of the desktop.
Displaying an object's context menu		Right click on the object. If the object is an open window, right click on the title bar. Context menus are often used to examine or modify an object's properties.

Operation	Button	Action
Resizing a window		Drag the size grip (lower right corner of window), or drag any window frame or corner.
Dragging an object		Hold a mouse button down on a selected object and move the mouse. Often, you can use either the left or right mouse buttons but they have different effects. To drop the object, release the mouse button.
Closing a window		Click the window's Close button.
Minimizing a window		Click the window's Minimize button.
Maximizing a window		Click the window's Maximize button.
Restoring a window to its pre-maximized size		Click the window's Restore button.
Moving an object		Select the object and then drag it to a new location.
Selecting multiple adjacent icons		Drag the mouse to form a selection rectangle which encloses the icons.
Selecting multiple nonadjacent icons		Select the first icon, then use CTRL + click on each additional icon.
Shutting down Windows		Choose Shut Down from the Taskbar's Start menu.
Opening an object		Double-click on the object.
Launching (running) a program		Choose the program's icon from the Taskbar's Start menu; or, double-click on the program's icon in an Explorer or My Computer window.
Switching between running programs		Select the Taskbar button of the program you want to switch to.
Closing (shutting down) a program		Click the program's Close button, or choose Exit (or Close) from the program's File menu.
Creating a new folder (subdirectory)		Right click in the area you want the new folder placed in; choose New and then choose Folder.
Copying objects.		Select the object(s), drag with the right mouse button to a new location, release the mouse button, and choose Copy Here from the context menu.
Moving objects.		Select the object(s), drag with the right mouse button to a new location, release the mouse button, and choose Move Here from the context menu.
Renaming objects.		Right click the object and choose Rename from the context menu.

Operation	Button	Action
Deleting objects.		Select the object(s) and drag them to the recycle bin; alternatively, select the object, right click, and choose Delete from the context menu.
Examining the contents of a disk or folder object		From within a My Computer or Explorer window, double-click on the object's icon
Changing window view styles	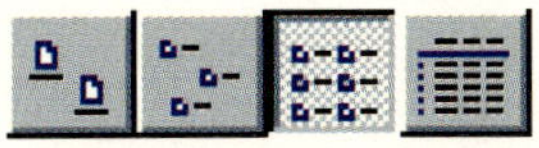	From within a My Computer or Explorer window, open the View menu, and choose Large Icons, Small Icons, List, or Details; alternatively, select one of the View buttons from the window's toolbar.
Displaying a View toolbar in Explorer or My Computer		Choose Toolbar from the View menu.
Arranging objects		From within the desktop, My Computer, or Explorer: right click a blank area, choose Arrange Icons from the context menu, and then pick from the list of arrangement options.

Glossary

address The name of an Internet location used to access the site directly.

All Folders pane Left half of the Explorer that displays drive and folder icon objects.

application program Program that uses a wide variety of features that are built in the operating system to provide a consistent interface to the user.

book An informational file that can be opened to reveal a list of topics as part of the Help feature.

byte Small units of information storage that are magnetically smeared across the surface of a disk or etched with a laser onto the underside of a CD-ROM.

cascading menu A menu like the Start menu whose submenus cascade, or flow, off main menu.

check box A window control that can be clicked on or off. In a group of check boxes, each box can be set independently.

click Method of selecting an object by positioning the pointer over an object and then pressing and immediately releasing either the left or right mouse button.

combo box A window control that combines a text box with a list box.

command button A window control that, when clicked, performs some action.

Contents pane Right half of the Explorer window that shows the files and folders in the current drive or folder.

copy To create a duplicate of a file in another location. The result of a copy process is two identical files with the same name in different places.

delete To move a file to the Recycle Bin.

desktop What the screen is meant to simulate in Windows. Such real-world metaphors make the system more intelligible to beginners.

Details view Displays information about each object's type and the date it was last modified.

document Any kind of data file—a letter, image, or other file that is created by an application program.

double-click Method of opening an object by positioning the pointer over the object and then pressing the left mouse button twice quickly and releasing it.

drag To hold down a mouse button and move the mouse while an object is selected.

drag and drop To select an object with the mouse and move, or drag, it across the desktop to a new location.

drop-down menu Opens when a menu title is selected from the menu bar and contains menu items.

file A collection of bytes. Computer hard drives are filled with thousands of files that make up the Windows operating system, application programs, and documents.

folder A Windows object that contains files and possibly other folders.

frame The border around a window.

group box A window control used extensively as a container to organize other controls. Normally, a group box is not manipulated, but the controls it contains are.

icon A graphical representation of an object in the Windows desktop.

Large Icons view The default view in My Computer that displays the objects as large icons.

launch Start a program.

list box A window control that displays a list of items that can be selected with the mouse.

List view Default view used in Explorer that automatically sorts files and folders by type and then alphabetically within each type group. Folders are displayed first and then files.

log on Required procedure to start Windows for users in a network environment. Logging on requires you to enter a user name and password to gain access to the computer system.

menu bar Part of a window located directly under the title bar that contains menu titles.

menu item Part of a pull-down menu that represents a command that can be selected to perform various actions.

menu title Appears in the menu bar and, when selected, opens a menu.

move To select a file and place it in a new location.

multitasking The ability to run numerous programs simultaneously, each in its own window.

network A group of computers that are joined together and can share devices like printers, disk drives, files, and other resources.

object Any part of the Windows desktop with which you perform unique actions.

operating system Provides an interface between the user and the computer.

option button A window control that can be clicked on or off. In a group of option buttons, only one option can be on at a time.

parent The folder at the top of the directory structure. Also called root.

pathname The full location and name of a file in the hierarchical structure of the system.

pop-up menu A menu that appears when an object is clicked with the right mouse button.

process A program that can run in a window, independent of other programs, allowing the user to be more productive.

program group items On the Programs menu, system tools that are indicated by a special program group icon. When you select this icon, further menus are revealed.

program items On the Programs menu, objects represented by miniature application program icons. When you select an icon, the program it represents will begin running.

rename To change the name of a file.

right-click To position the pointer over an object and press the right mouse button to display a pop-up menu.

root The folder at the top of the directory structure. Also called parent.

scroll bar A window control used to change the view of a document that is larger than can be seen in the viewing window.

shell A powerful, advanced user interface that allows visual exploration of Windows 95.

size grip A special handle that appears in the lower-right corner of a window and can be used to resize the window.

slider A window control used to adjust the magnitude of certain settings whose numerical description may not be easily understood.

Small Icons view Displays objects as small icons that are similar to the icons displayed in a window title bar.

spin box A window control that contains a value (such as the amount of indent at the left margin) and arrows on its right side. Clicking the arrows causes the value in the box to change.

status bar Appears at the bottom of a window and is used to display important information about the window or program.

tab A window control used to organize different pages, or panels, of controls. Clicking a tab brings its page into view, where you can then manipulate its controls. Tabs make it possible for menus to be shallower (have a shorter series of choices).

text box A window control in which you to type text of your choice or edit text already in the text box. Also called an edit box.

title text Caption within the title bar that identifies the window.

toolbar A row of buttons that are sometimes present in a window.

toolbox A collection of icons that appear in application programs, such as Paint, along the left side of the window. The icons give you quick access to commonly needed tools.

topic An informational file that can be opened and read as part of the Help feature.

tree Term used to describe a directory structure.

window Overlapping rectangular area on-screen that can contain its own program.

Index

Accessories, 24, 25
All Folders pane, 50
Applications. *See also* Programs
  accessing. *See* Launching applications
  described, 1
  switching between, 31–32
  in Taskbar, 4, 5
  using multiple, simultaneously, 30
Arrow, mouse pointer as, 19
Audio CD player, 4, 5

Bitmap files, 26, 29–30
Borders, window, 9
Buttons
  in dialog boxes, 16
  on mouse, 5–8
  in Taskbar, 4–5, 28, 32–33
  for window control, 9–13
Cascading menus, 24, 25
Check boxes, 16
Clicking, 6–8, 46
Clock, 4, 5
Closing windows, 12
Collapse, 51, 52
Color, 30
Combo boxes, 17
Command buttons, 16
Commands
  in menus. *See* Menus
  undoing, 55
Contents page (Help), 19–20
Contents pane (Explorer), 50
Context-sensitive Help, 17–18
Controls, 15–17
Copying files and folders, 43–45, 49, 54–55
(CTRL), 47
Cut, 49, 54–55

Deleting files and folders, 4, 46–48, 55
Desktop, 3–5
Details, 53
Dialog boxes, 16–17
Dial-Up Networking, 36
Directories, 39–39, 51
Disconnect Network Drive, 54
Disk drives, 37–38, 52
Documents. *See also* Files
  opening, 29–30
  overview, 29
  recently accessed, list of, 26
DOS programs, running, 26
Double-clicking, 7–8
Drag and drop, 43–44
Dragging, 9
Drives. *See* Disk drives

Edit boxes, 16
E-mail, 4
Exiting Microsoft Windows, 8
Expand, 51, 52
Explorer. *See* Microsoft, Explorer
Extensions, file, 26

Files
  data files. *See* Documents
  extensions, 26
  finding, 26
  folders vs., 38, 43
  managing. *See* Microsoft, Explorer; My Computer
  overview, 36
  system of, 37–39
Finding
  files and folders, 26
  Help information, 20
Folders. *See also* Files
  files vs., 38, 43
  managing. *See* Microsoft Explorer; My Computer
  navigating, 30
  overview, 38

Go to a Different Folder, 54
Graphical user interface (GUI), 1, 2
Group boxes, 16

Hard disks. *See* Disk drives
Help
  via Contents page, 19–20
  context-sensitive, 17–18
  via Index page, 20
  overview, 17
  searching for, 20
  system for, accessing, 18–19, 26
  Tooltips, 18

Icons, 3, 8, 53
Inbox, 4
Index page (Help), 20

Large Icons, 8, 53
Launching applications
  by double–clicking, 7, 40
  from Start menu, 5, 27–28
List boxes, 17
List view, 53

Map Network Drive, 54
Maximize, 12, 13
Menus
  cascading menus, 24
  pull-down menus, 13
  menu bars, 9, 13–14
  popup menus, 5–6
  selecting, 13–14
Microsoft
  Exchange, 4
  Explorer
  accessing, 50–51
  changing folder access, 54
  changing view of, 53
  My Computer vs., 40–41, 50
  navigating file/folder structure, 51–52
  opening drives and folders, 52
  overview, 50
  Toolbar for, 53
  Windows. *See also specific component or function*
    configuring, 26
    exiting, 8, 26
    overview, 2
    starting, 2
Minimize, 12–13
Mouse
  buttons, using, 5–8
  double-clicking, 7–8
  dragging, 9–10
  moving, 5
  overview, 5
  pointer, 10, 19
Moving
  files and folders, 45
  windows, 11
  Multitasking, 30
  Music files, 41
  My Computer
  copying files and folders, 43–45, 49
  creating files, 41–43
  creating folders, 43
  cutting and pasting files, 49
  deleting files and folders, 4, 46–48
  Explorer vs., 40–41, 50
  icon for, 4
  launching programs, 40
  moving files and folders, 45
  navigating multiple windows, 40–41
  opening, 37
  opening folders, 39
  overview, 36
  renaming files and folders, 45–46

Naming files and folders, 45–46
Networking
  browsing resources. with Network Neighborhood, 4
  Dial-Up Networking, 36
  Network Drive buttons, 54
  New, 43
  Notepad, 40

Objects, desktop, 3
Opening
  applications. *See* Launching applications
  documents, 29–30
  folders, 39
Operating systems, 1
Option buttons, 16

Paint, 28, 29–30
Paste, 49, 54–55
Pointer, mouse, 10. *See also* Mouse
Processes, in windows, 2
Programs
  applications. *See* Applications
  list of, accessing, 24–26
  operating systems, 1
  program groups, 24, 25
  shell programs, 2
Programs (menu item), 24–26
Push buttons, 16

Radio buttons, 16
Recycle Bin, 4, 46–48
Restore button, 12, 13
Run, 26

Scrolling, 16
Searching. *See* Finding
Settings, 26
Shell, Windows as, 2
Shut Down, 8, 26
Size grip, 9
Sizing windows, 9–10, 12–13
Sliders, 17
Small Icons view, 53
Sound files, 41
Spin boxes, 17
Start menu
  accessing, 23
  button for, 5, 23
  options, 24–26
  overview, 24
Status area, 4, 5
Status bars, 9, 14–15

Tab boxes, 17
Taskbar, 4–5, 28, 32–33
Text boxes, 16
Text files. *See* Documents
Title bar, 9, 10–11
Toolboxes, 28
Tooltips, 18
Trackbars, 17
Tree, directory, 38–39, 51

Undo, 55
Up One Level, 54

Video Play (Help), 20
View styles, 53

WAV files, 41
What's This? button, 30
Windows
  closing, 12
  components of, 9
  controls for, 15–17
  described, 1–2
  frames, 9
  information about, displaying, 14–15
  moving, 11
  navigating, 40–41, 51–52
  sizing, 9–10, 12–13
Windows environment. *See* Microsoft, Windows
WordPad, 31
Word processors, 31